BETTER PICTURE GUIDE TO
Photographing Nudes

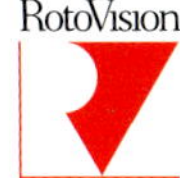

A RotoVision Book
Published and Distributed by RotoVision SA
Rue Du Bugnon 7
1299 Crans-Près-Céligny
Switzerland

RotoVision SA, Sales & Production Office
Sheridan House, 112/116A Western Road
Hove, East Sussex BN3 1DD, UK

Tel: +44 (0) 1273 72 72 68
Fax: +44 (0) 1273 72 72 69
E-mail: sales@RotoVision.com
Website: www.rotovision.com

Distributed to the trade in the United States by:
Watson-Guptill Publications
1515 Broadway
New York, NY 10036

ISBN 2-88046-516-8

Book design by Brenda Dermody
Diagrams by Austin Carey

Production and separations in Singapore by ProVision Pte. Ltd.
Tel: +65 334 7720
Fax: +65 334 7721

BETTER PICTURE GUIDE TO

Photographing Nudes

DAVID DAYE

Contents

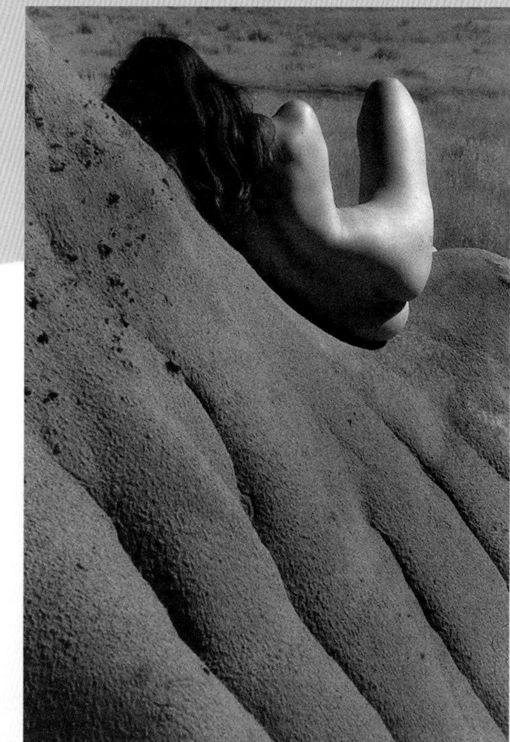

Composing the Image

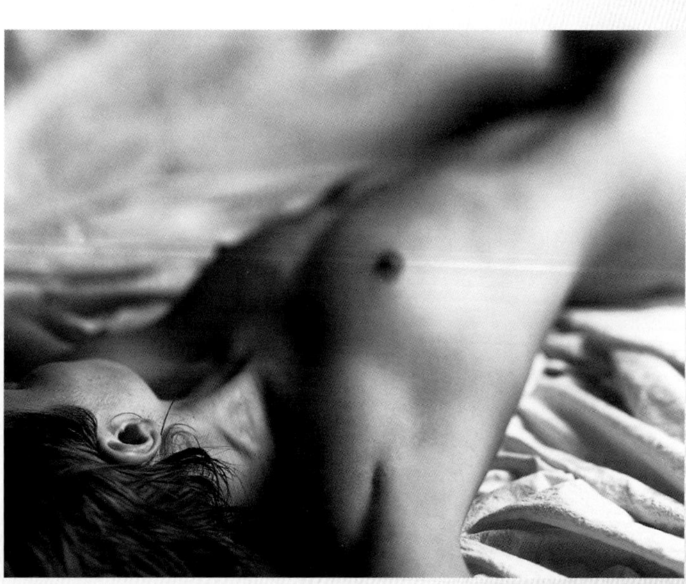

I

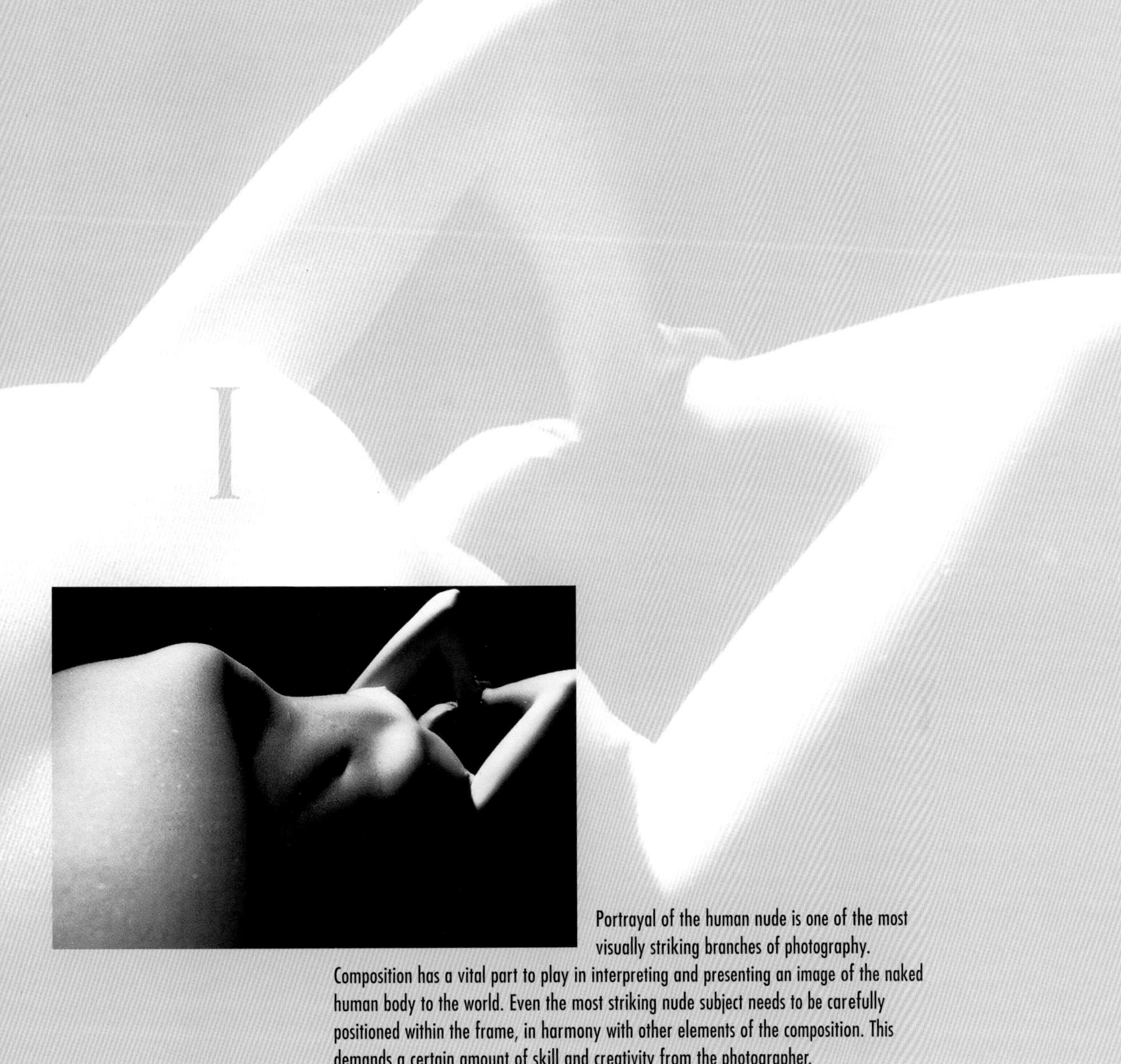

Portrayal of the human nude is one of the most visually striking branches of photography. Composition has a vital part to play in interpreting and presenting an image of the naked human body to the world. Even the most striking nude subject needs to be carefully positioned within the frame, in harmony with other elements of the composition. This demands a certain amount of skill and creativity from the photographer.

The Golden Section

The golden section, or rule of thirds, is a classic compositional device. Imagine a grid of lines splitting the frame into three equal sections both horizontally and vertically. Placing the subject at one of the points where these imaginary lines intersect will give a pleasing, well-balanced composition.

Seeing

Photographer Eric Boutilier-Brown used an attractive landscape setting as a backdrop for this outdoor nude study. By placing the nude model within the landscape, he aimed to create a picture that would evoke classical depictions of goddesses such as Venus and Aphrodite in natural settings.

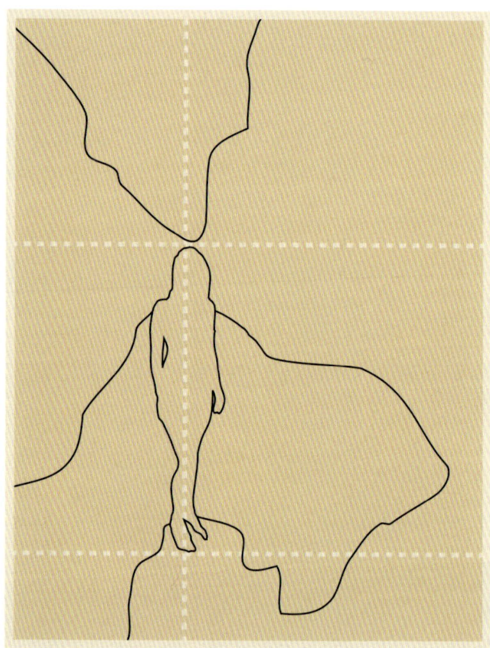

Thinking

The location and the rock in the stream provided the photographer with a ready-made situation for this well-balanced composition. He positioned the model roughly a third of the way in from the edge of the frame and a third of the way up from the bottom. The stream behind her serves to lead the eye into the frame towards the distant mountain.

Acting

No external lighting controls were required in these bright, overcast conditions. The picture was taken with a medium format camera, ensuring plenty of detail both on the model's body and in the landscape around her. The photographer used a wide-angle lens to impart a sense of depth and drama, while a slow shutter speed blurred the running water of the stream, conveying a sense of movement.

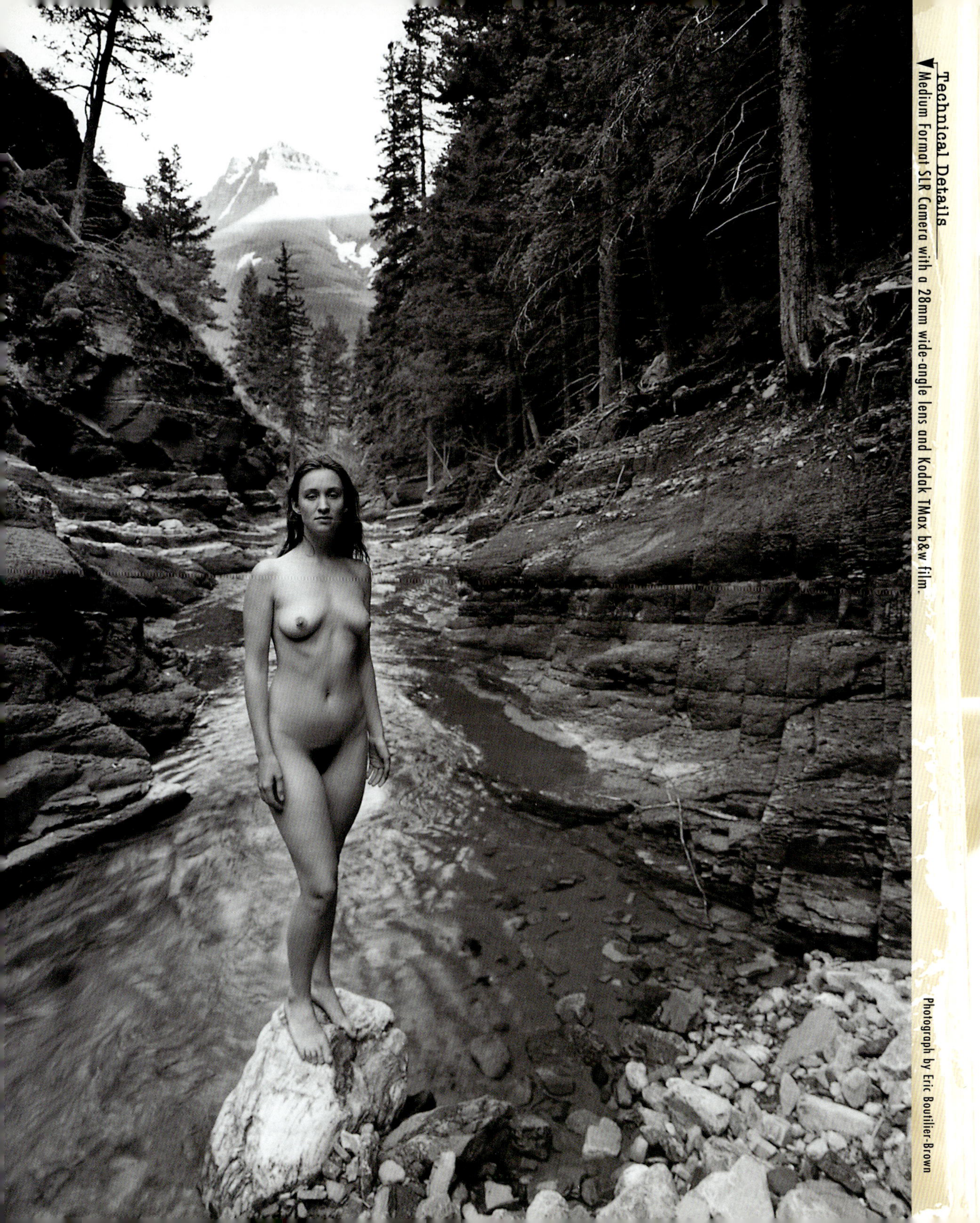

Technical Details

Medium Format SLR Camera with a 28mm wide-angle lens and Kodak TMax b&w film.

Photograph by Eric Boutilier-Brown

Leading the Eye

Highlighting a particular element within the frame can create a strong first point of visual contact. Careful arrangement of the subject within the frame leads the eye into the composition, giving an impression of depth. Exploiting the characteristics of equipment such as wide-angle lenses can exaggerate the effect.

Seeing

The photographer wanted to exploit the fact that an object that is close to the lens automatically appears closer to the viewer. This produces an almost 3-D effect that creates instant visual impact.

Thinking

To create a dramatic feeling of depth, he filled a large part of the frame with the model's body. He posed the model so that her leg appeared almost to be breaking out of the picture area. By adopting a close shooting position he exaggerated the effect.

aActing

The photographer used an extreme wide-angle lens, which creates a dramatically distorted view of the human body, especially when it is viewed close up. The strange perspective nevertheless provides a path into the picture for the eye to follow. At the same time, the lens's characteristically wide depth of field means that the picture is largely sharp from front to back.

Technical Details

35mm SLR Camera with a 19mm wide-angle lens and Kodak High Speed Infrared b&w film.

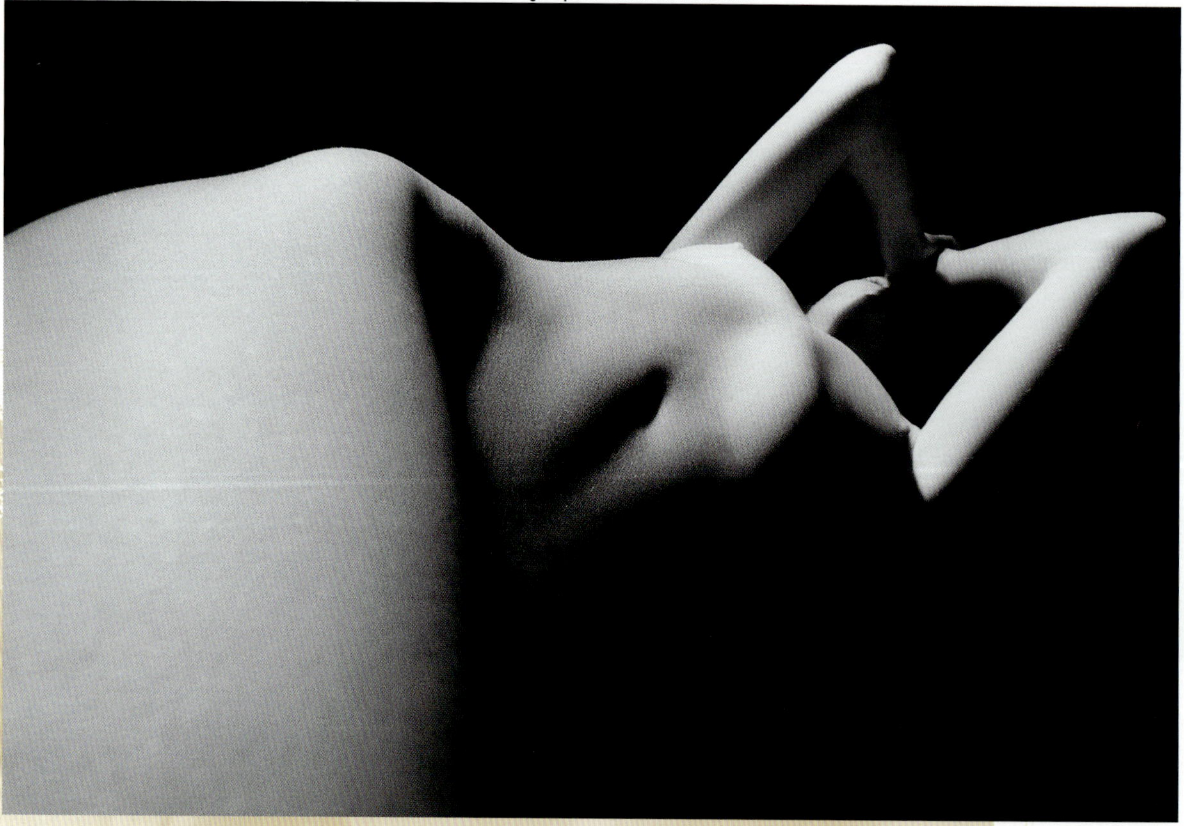

Photograph by Eric Boutilier-Brown

Technical Details

35mm SLR Camera with a 20mm wide-angle lens and Kodak High Speed Infrared b&w film.

Again the photographer exploited the characteristics of an extreme wide-angle lens. The fact that the girl's foot is so much larger in proportion to the rest of her body catches the viewer's attention. At second glance it seems more natural when we see the rest of the body, and our eye is led naturally into the image.

Photograph by Eric Boutilier-Brown

Framing the Image

The skill of composition lies in selecting an angle of view that highlights the subject while cutting out the inevitable mass of extraneous detail that surrounds it. This is done by placing the subject carefully within the field of vision of the particular camera and lens combination being used, and can be refined by selecting lenses with wider or narrower angles of view. Composition can be greatly enhanced by placing the subject within a naturally occurring frame created by physical objects. Doors, windows and the branches of trees all make good natural frames.

Technical Details

35mm SLR Camera with an 85mm short telephoto lens and Fujichrome Astia film rated at ISO 80.

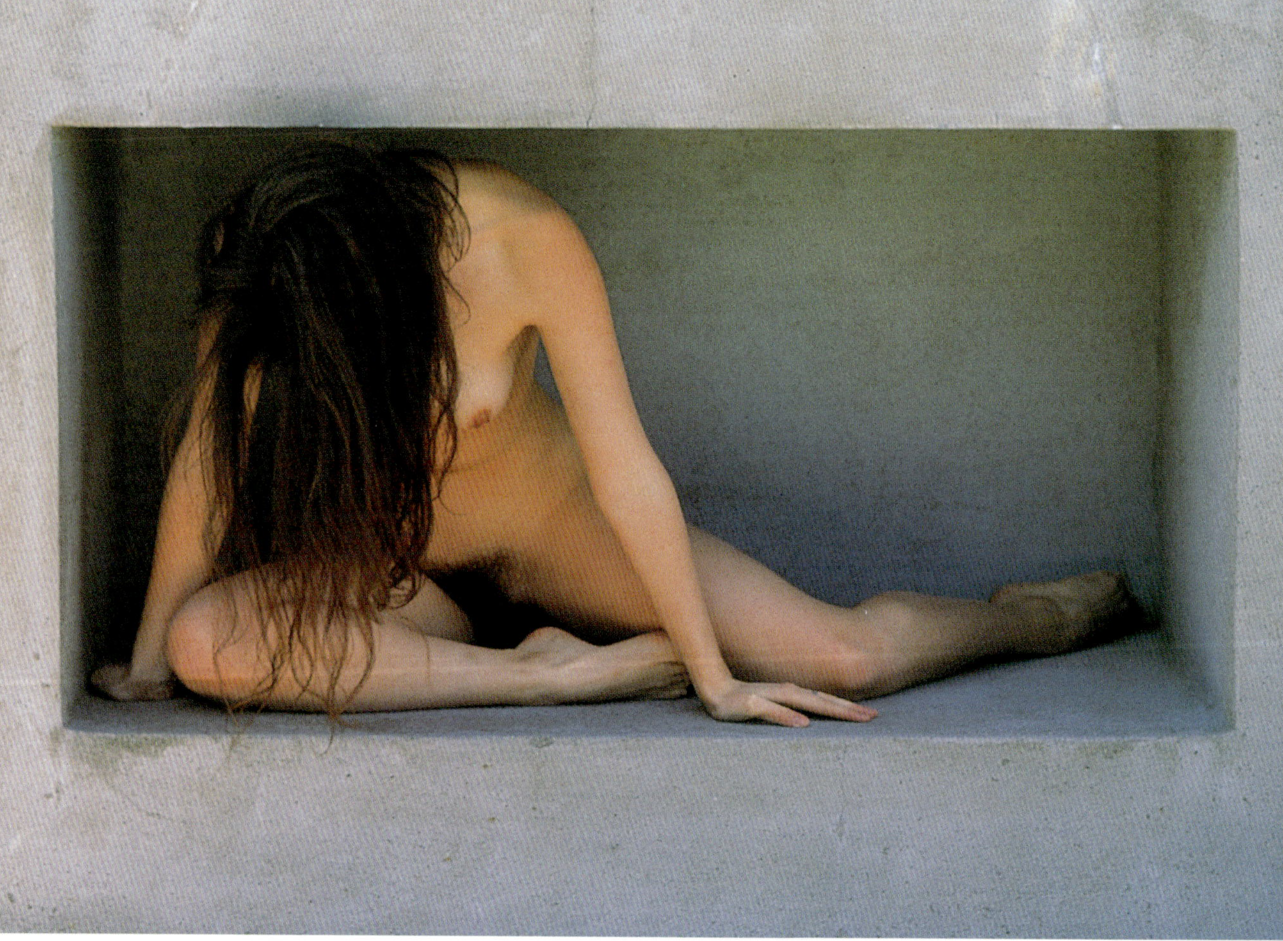

Photograph by Eric Boutilier-Brown

Seeing

The most obvious frame of all is the film frame that contains the image, whether it is rectangular, square or panoramic. Here, however, Eric Boutilier-Brown made use of a man-made concrete shelf to create a frame within a frame.

Thinking

The proportions of the concrete shelf almost exactly match those of the 35mm film frame. This allowed the photographer to crop in tightly while keeping an even area of frame all around the subject. He placed the model off-centre with one leg extended, providing an almost perfect example of how the rule of thirds can be used to create a balanced composition.

Acting

The scene was lit by natural daylight, which was strong though not falling directly on the subject, who was shielded by the concrete structure. The photographer used a reflector placed on the ground in front of her to throw light into the concrete space, illuminating both the model and the background evenly.

The panoramic frame is narrower than a conventional rectangular image frame. In 35mm cameras which have this facility it is created by a mask that crops out an area so as to make an elongated image frame. This is effective with subjects such as landscapes and with those that have horizontal elements.

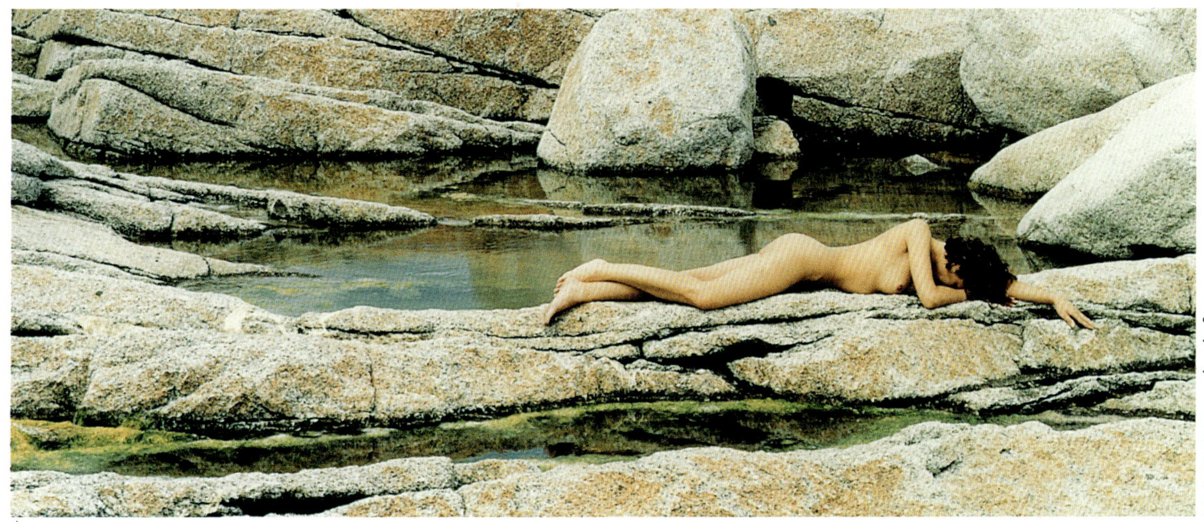

Photograph by Eric Boutilier-Brown

Technical Details

Medium Format Camera with a 6x12cm film back and a 120mm telephoto lens, and Kodak PRN film.

Shape & Form

The nude model is of course a living, breathing human being but, treated as a still life, the human body can be the source of photographic images that are almost abstract in nature. Bold framing and imaginative use of lighting can highlight shapes and patterns that might not be immediately apparent in a conventional nude study.

Seeing

Here the photographer wanted to use the natural contours of the human form to create an essentially abstract composition. He chose strong, directional studio lighting that would concentrate attention on the shape of the model's body.

Thinking

Instead of looking at the whole figure he concentrated on a specific section. He used the lighting to enhance the contrast between light and dark areas, ensuring that the model's torso stood out clearly from the background, which was thrown into shadow.

Acting

Two softboxes were used for this image. The first was pointed straight at the subject, while the second light was positioned at an angle to the model's body.

The quality of the available lighting produced soft shadows despite the high contrast.
The subject's form is clearly and dramatically defined where the light and the dark areas meet.

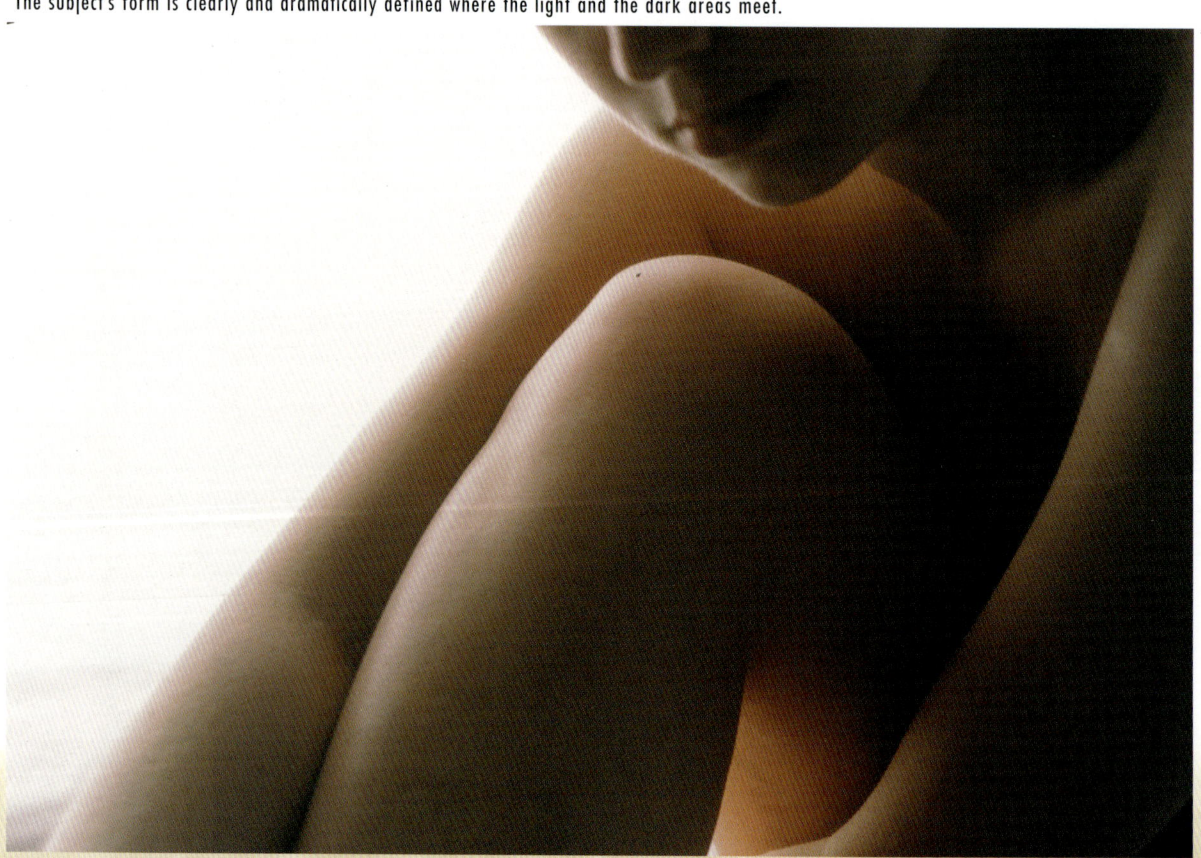

Technical Details
35mm SLR Camera with an 85mm lens and ISO 400 slide film.

Photograph by Eric Boutilier-Brown

Technical Details

6x6cm Medium Format Camera with a 150mm lens and Agfa APX 100 b&w film.

Photograph by Eric Boutilier-Brown

Using Texture

Human skin has a texture all of its own. This can be highlighted in close-up compositions or juxtaposed with the textures of other objects, either natural or man-made, to create effective contrasts. In a natural landscape, rocks, earth, wood and tree bark provide great potential for contrasting textures. If using man-made textures, fabrics, furniture, painted walls, bricks, concrete and metal structures are just a few of the possibilities.

Technical Details

Medium Format SLR Camera with a 50mm wide-angle lens and Kodak TMax b&w film.

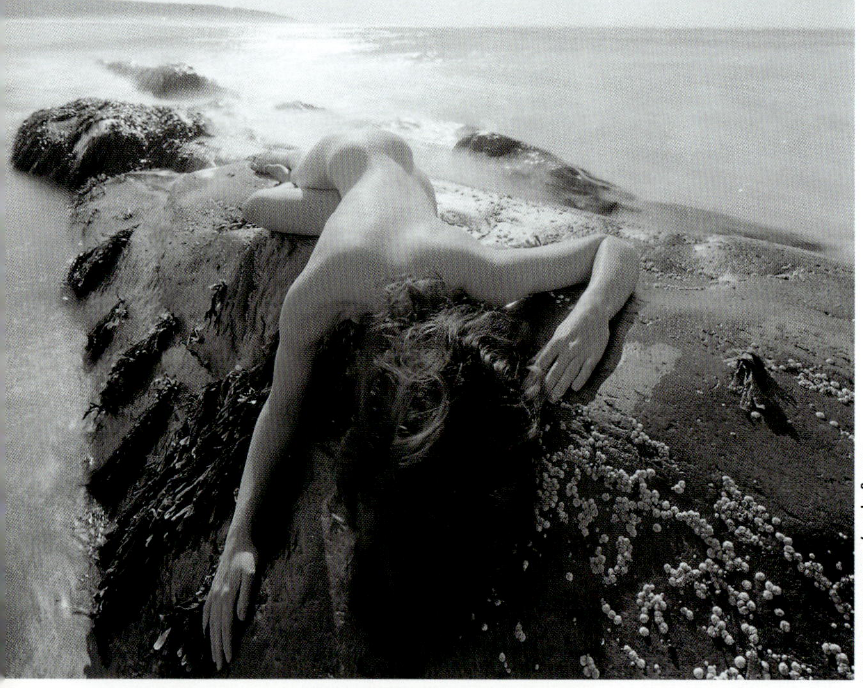

Photograph by Eric Boutilier-Brown

Soft and rough textures are effectively mixed in this image. The model's smooth skin and the jagged nature of the barnacles are contrasting elements that immediately grab the viewer's attention.

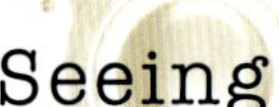

Seeing

The focus of this composition is on shape and texture, with the photographer concentrating on the contrasts between the textures of the model's hair and smooth skin and the rough, sandy texture of the rock. Many natural surfaces can be used to provide an effective contrast with human skin.

Thinking

As the photographer wanted a semi-abstract image, he posed the model so that her face could not be seen, as this might have distracted attention from the shapes and textures on which he wanted to concentrate. To reinforce the abstract theme, he asked her to adopt a pose that echoed the deep fissures in the natural rock.

Acting

The photographer used an extreme wide-angle lens to give depth to the picture. He shot in the middle of the day so that the strong sunlight brought out the textures of skin and rock more dramatically. The bright daylight also ensured that the lens's smallest aperture could be used, giving the maximum depth of field.

Technical Details

35mm SLR Camera with a 20mm wide-angle lens and Kodak High Speed Infrared b&w film.

Photograph by Eric Boutilier-Brown

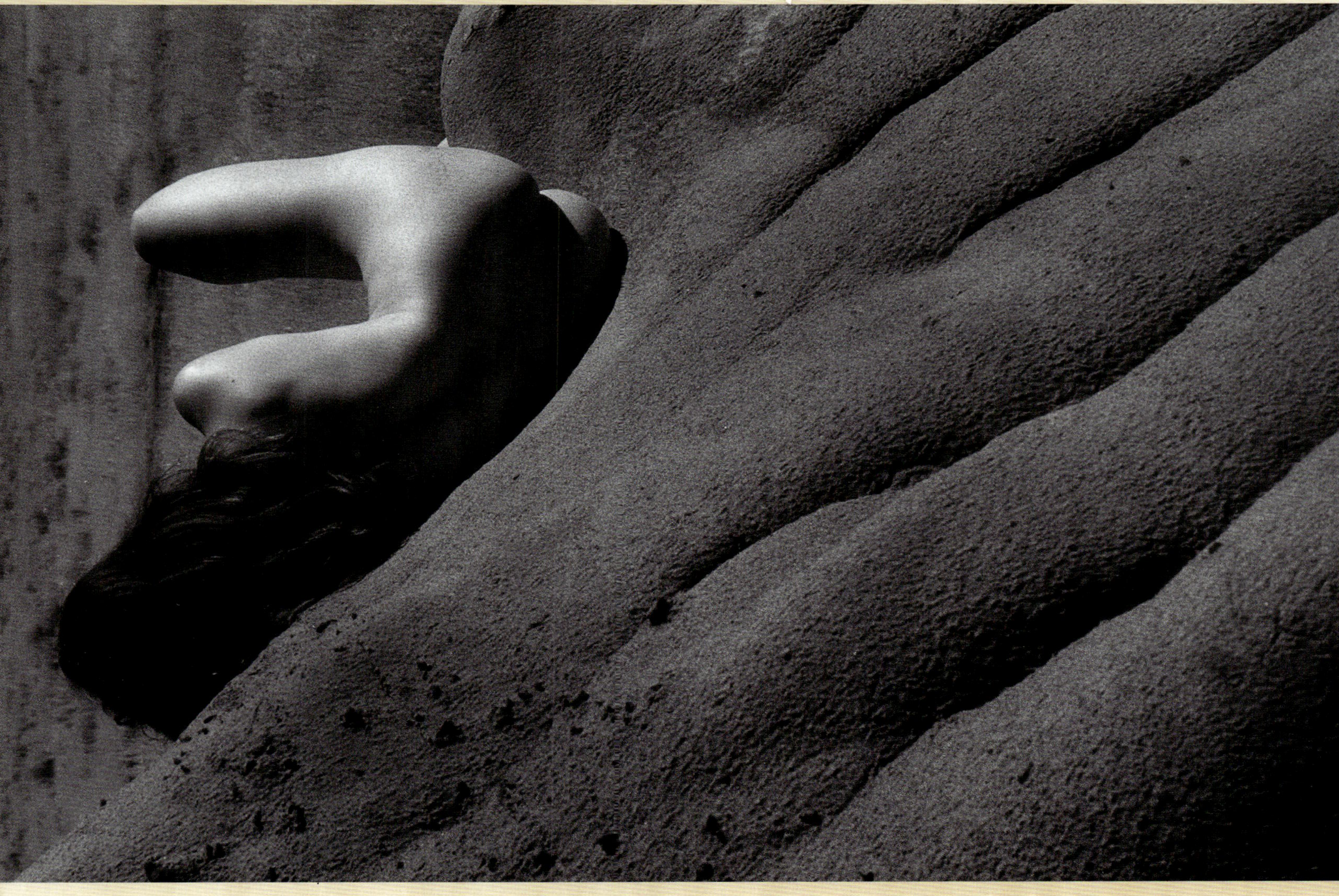

Dramatic Diagonals

When a subject is positioned across the diagonal of a frame instead of being horizontally or vertically aligned it produces a dynamic visual effect. A diagonal composition encourages the viewer to look at the overall shape of the image first before appreciating the details within it.

Technical Details

Medium Format SLR Camera with a 120mm telephoto lens and Kodak TMax b&w film.

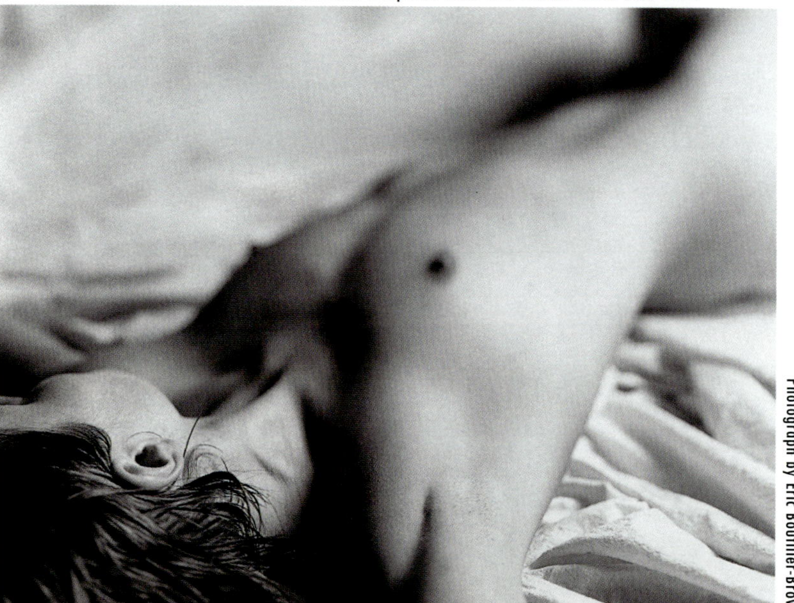

Photograph by Eric Boutilier-Brown

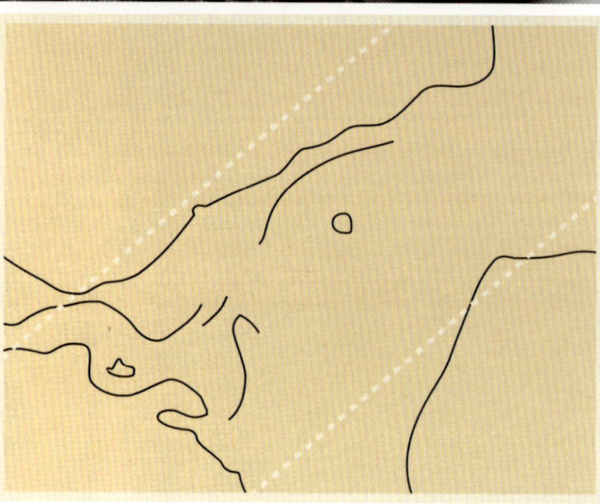

Like the photograph on the right, this image is aligned from the bottom left to the top right of the frame, creating a strong diagonal.

Seeing

The photographer placed the model diagonally in the frame to create an almost abstract image. The background is simple but impact is created by the organic shape of the model's body being incorporated into a strongly geometric composition. The effect is completed by bold lighting which creates complementary areas of light and dark.

Thinking

The composition is finely balanced. The photographer aligned the elements of the picture so that they aimed towards the corners of the frame, creating a sense of tension.

Acting

The camera was tilted so that the line created by the woman's torso and right leg travelled from the top right to the bottom left of the frame. Illumination was provided by available natural light. A wide-angle lens exaggerated the feeling of vertigo.

Technical Details

35mm SLR Camera with a 20mm wide-angle lens and Fujichrome Sensia ISO 400 slide film.

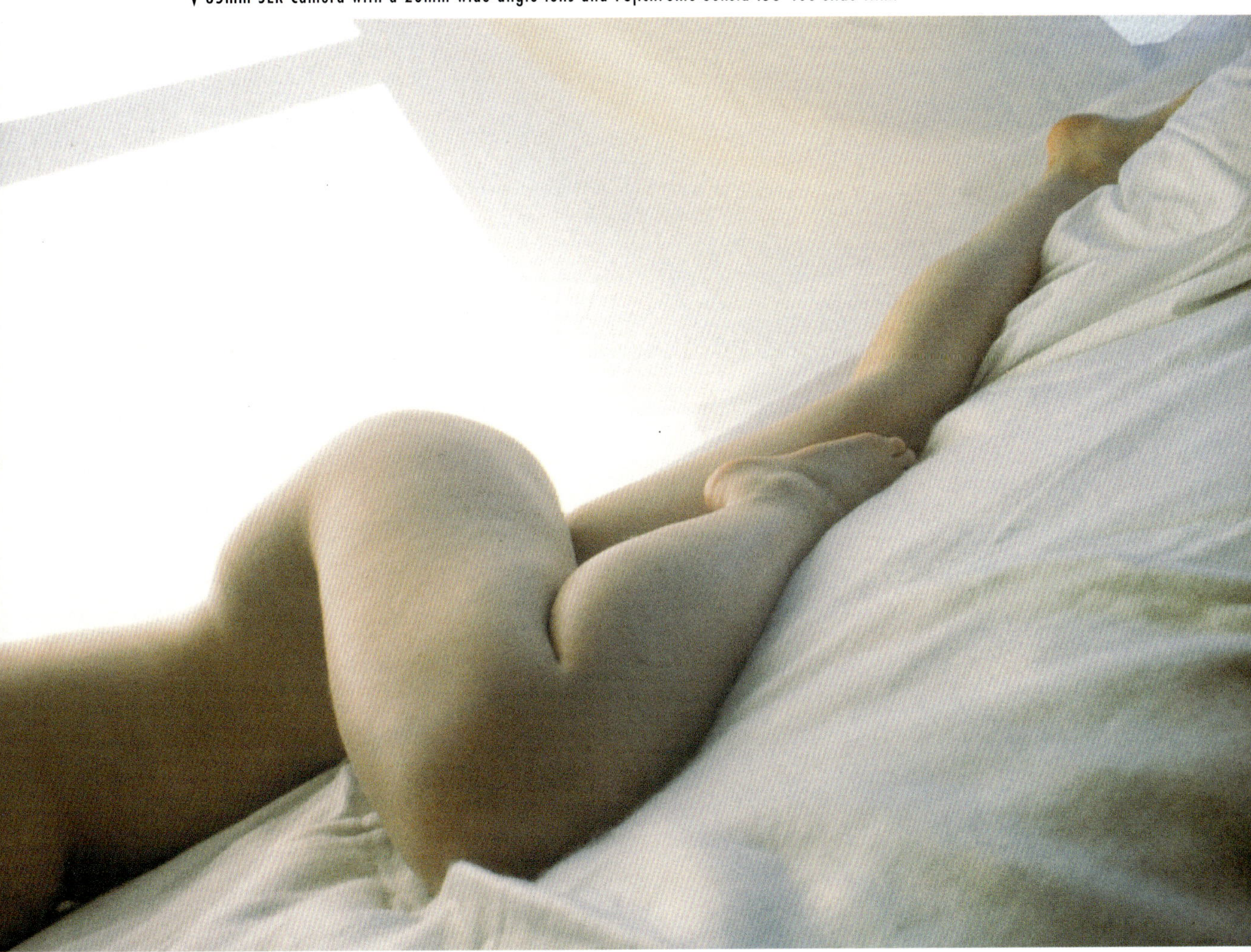

Photograph by Eric Boutilier-Brown

Dramatic Diagonals

Seeing

Eric Boutilier-Brown used a diagonal composition to make the most of the elements at his disposal. If the figure had been positioned vertically in the frame the composition would have been a much more rigid, static arrangement.

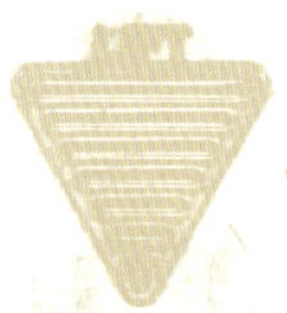

Thinking

Horizon lines, whether shown within the frame or implied, usually help the viewer to align an image before assessing its qualities as a composition. Here the photographer framed the image so that there was no obvious horizon line, creating a feeling of space and depth and concentrating attention on the shapes and relative positions of the various elements.

Acting

The feeling of depth was enhanced by the use of a wide-angle lens, which helped create dramatic perspectives and gave front-to-back depth of field. Boutilier-Brown used infrared film, which gave an ethereal glow to the model's skin and made the already dramatic cloud formation stand out boldly against the sky.

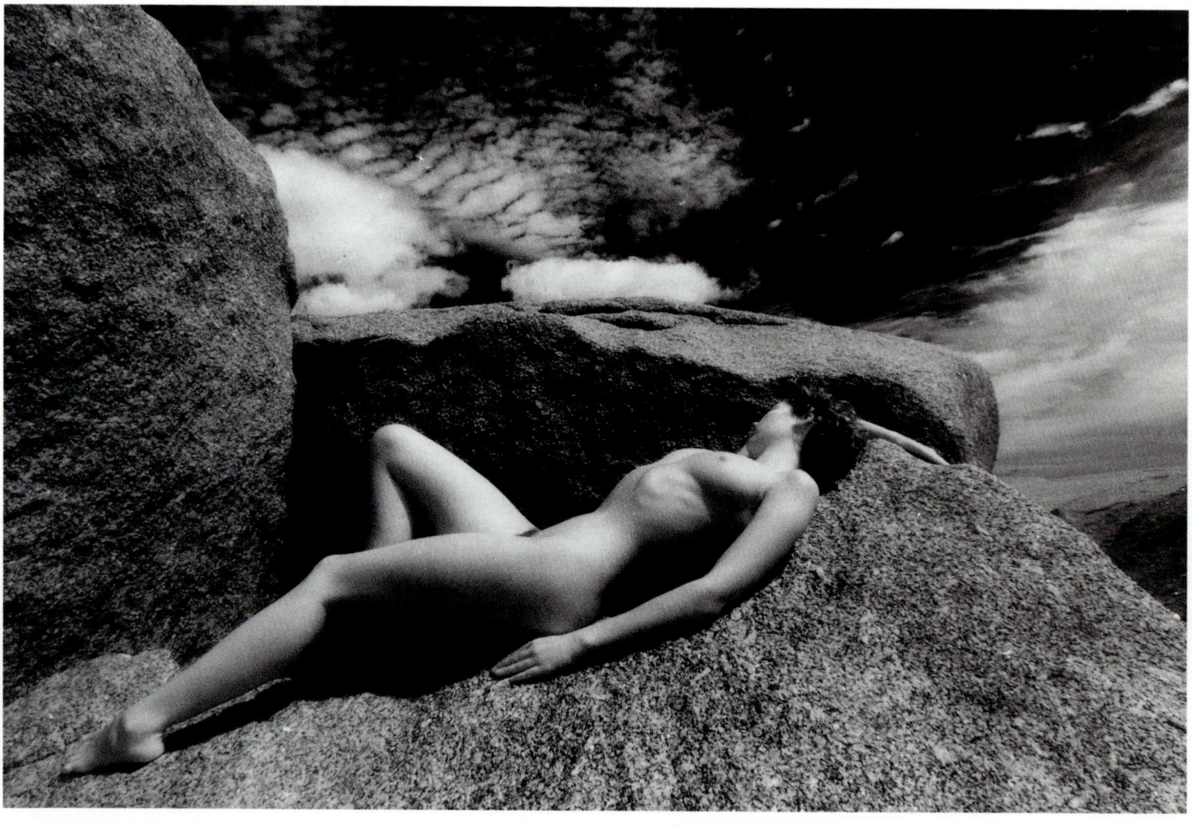

Technical Details

35mm SLR Camera with a 20mm wide-angle lens and Kodak High Speed Infrared b&w film.

Photograph by Eric Boutilier-Brown

Technical Details

Medium Format SLR Camera with a 50mm wide-angle lens and Kodak TMax ISO 100 b&w film.

The wide-angle lens, combined with a low viewpoint, has made the model's extended right leg seem even longer. The strong diagonal line created by her body is balanced by the alignment of the horizon line, as implied by the reflected trees along the top edge of the image frame. The photographer used a softer natural setting for his model in this shot, but the diagonal composition still creates a sense of drama.

Photograph by Eric Boutilier-Brown

Symmetrical Composition

Symmetrical composition creates a sense of balance in a picture and is generally pleasing to the eye. Symmetry can be created by imaginative placing of props or by seeking out complementary elements of a natural landscape and positioning the model carefully between them. Symmetry need not rely on physical objects alone: complementary areas of light and dark can also be used to create balanced compositions.

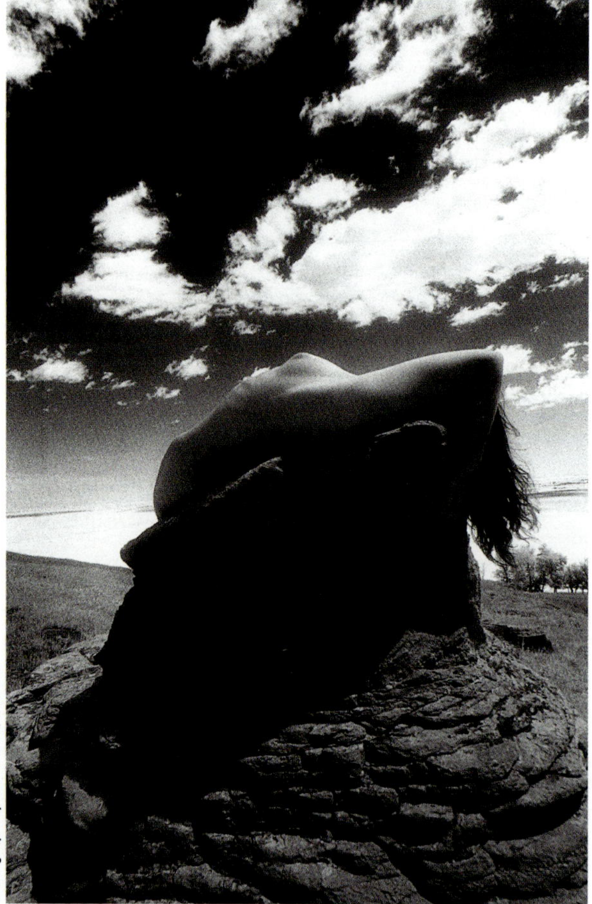

Photograph by Eric Boutilier-Brown

The subject was positioned in the centre of the frame. The cloud-filled sky and the rock the girl is resting on provide areas of interest above and below the figure, giving a visual balance to the image. The very wide viewing angle of the lens that was used encompassed large areas of peripheral detail but the photographer has successfully incorporated these into the image. He used these to balance one another out. He exaggerated the angle of view by using a panoramic film back and tilting it on its side.

Seeing

Nature offers many examples of symmetry that can be exploited by the observant photographer. The arrangement of the rocky location and the water was a perfect setting for this symmetrical composition.

Thinking

Having assessed the location, the photographer realised that the apex of the triangle formed by the water was a natural place to position the subject, as it created a balanced composition. On a different level, the presence of the nude figure softens the hard appearance of the rocks. He was also keen to exploit the contrast between the soft and seemingly fragile human body and the solid mass of the slabs of rock.

Acting

The image needed careful framing. As he was using a 35mm SLR camera, the photographer was able to adjust his composition while assessing the angle of view directly through the lens. He ensured that the scene was framed exactly how he wanted it by using a tripod that held the camera solidly in place.

Technical Details

Medium Format SLR Camera and Kodak TMax b&w film.

Technical Details

5x4 Large Format Camera with a 210mm lens and Kodak TMax b&w film.

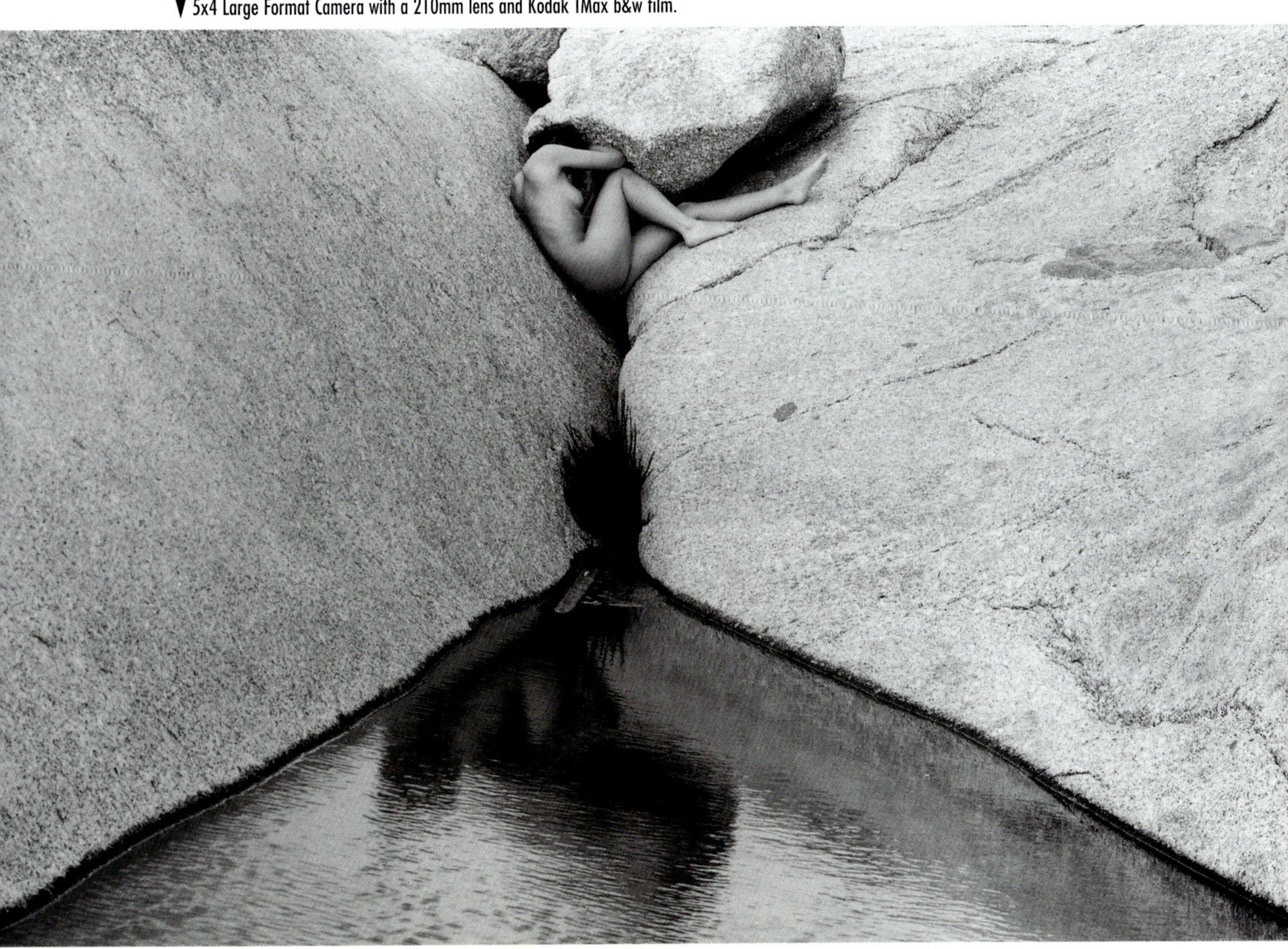

Photograph by Eric Boutilier-Brown

Asymmetrical Composition

Asymmetrical composition creates tension between the different elements within the frame and imparts a sense of drama to the image. It can be achieved by placing the main subject off-centre or by focusing attention on a particular part of the model's body. Equally, bold lighting can be used to create areas of light and dark that emphasise a particular part of the frame at the expense of others.

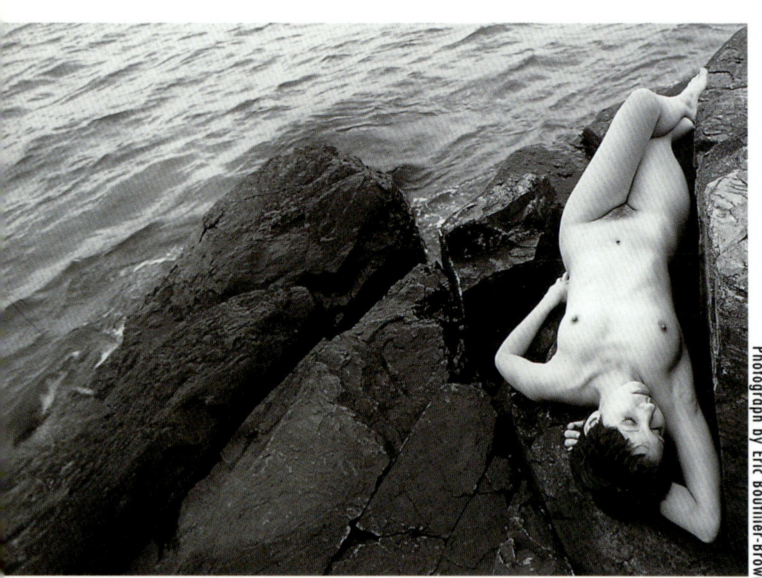

Photograph by Eric Boutilier-Brown

Technical Details

35mm SLR Camera with a 20mm wide-angle lens and Kodak TMax b&w film.

The off-centre positioning of the figure is balanced by the rocks and the water. These fill the remaining space in the frame, provide additional textures and echo the shape of the nude, putting the whole image into context.

Seeing

The photographer deliberately placed the subject off-centre. There is no obvious focal point in the image yet it's an effective composition. The curve created by the curled-up figure makes a strong, distinctive shape.

Thinking

The photographer used a combination of high contrast and shadow areas, together with the pose itself, to create a strong sense of atmosphere. He framed the figure so that it dominates and fills most of the image area.

Acting

A telephoto lens allowed the photographer to crop in close on the contours of the model's body. He used studio flash to light the shot, but recreated the effect of window light by placing a frame in front of the flashgun to cast shadows across the subject.

Technical Details

Medium Format SLR Camera with a 210mm telephoto lens and Kodak TMax b&w film.

Photograph by Eric Boutilier-Brown

Asymmetrical Composition

Seeing

Eric Boutilier-Brown chose to disregard conventional notions of composition in this studio shot by concentrating attention on the left-hand side of the frame. Together with the unusual framing, he made use of strongly contrasting areas of light and dark to create a sense of drama.

Thinking

Working in the studio, the photographer had time to try out different poses. The medium format camera he used calls for more deliberate framing than is normally the case with a 35mm camera, which can be hand-held and therefore allows for more spontaneous poses.

Acting

The photographer used a telephoto lens to frame the subject tightly. He arranged the stark studio lighting so that it picked out her face and torso, leaving the rest of the frame in deep shadow. He used the camera's precise focusing capabilities to draw the viewer's attention to the model's breasts.

Technical Details

Medium Format SLR Camera with a 120mm telephoto lens and Kodak TMax b&w film.

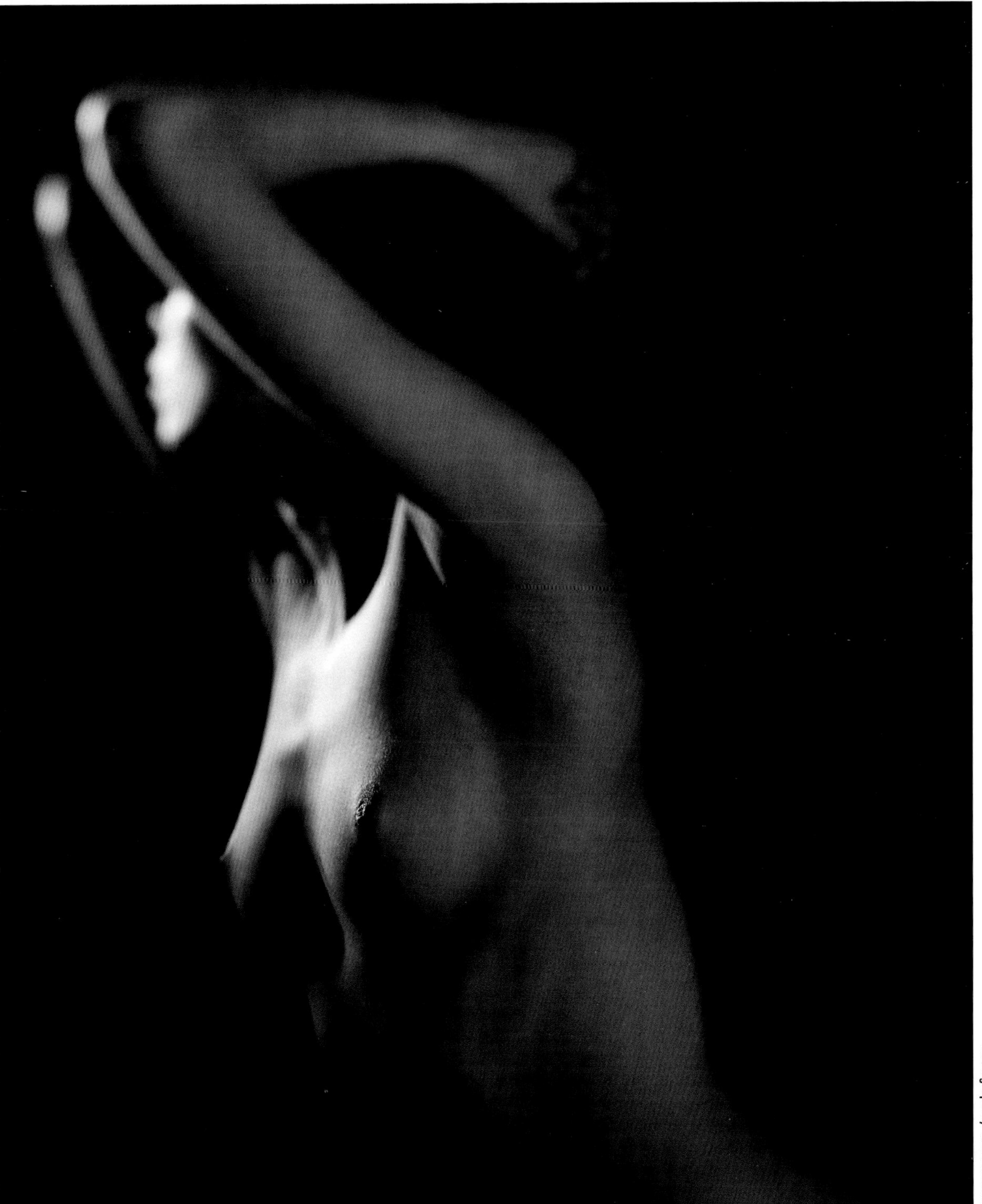

Photograph by Eric Boutilier-Brown

The Detail Shot

Cropping in close on a part of the model's body creates images that are full of impact. A detail shot can highlight shape and texture and is particularly suited to the use of dramatic lighting. Detail shots can be abstract in nature although they still recognisably portray a part of the human body.

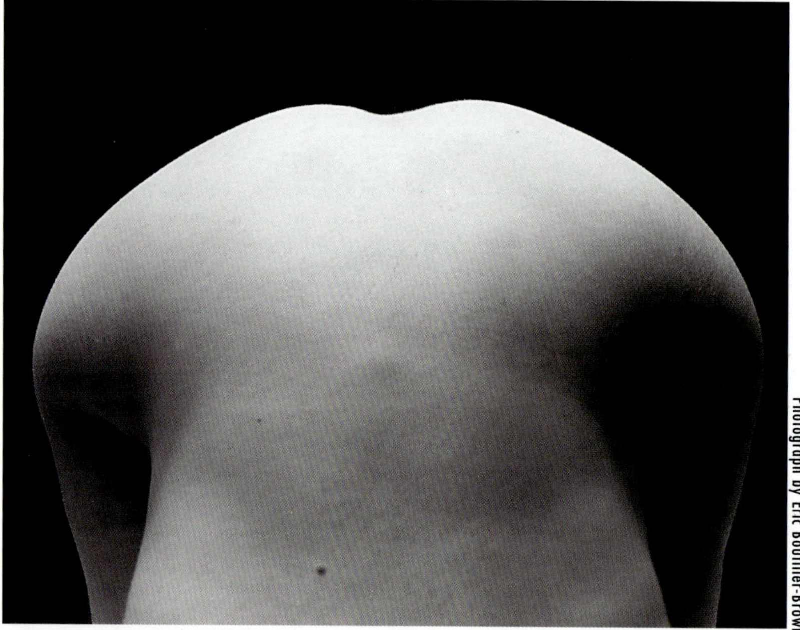

Photograph by Eric Boutilier-Brown

Technical Details
Medium Format SLR Camera with a 210mm telephoto lens and Kodak TMax b&w film.

Seeing

Eric Boutilier-Brown wanted to isolate a small part of the model's body. This creates a totally different view of a familiar subject. We know which part of the body this is, yet photographed in this way it takes on a new character.

Thinking

He placed the model in an unusual pose and photographed her from an unconventional viewpoint. He aimed to create a semi-abstract image in which symmetry was a key element. A photograph with just the right amount of detail may be sufficient to suggest the position and alignment of the rest of the body, which we cannot see.

Acting

The photographer positioned a studio flash above the model's stooped torso to emphasise the curve created by her bottom and hips. The large format film has made the most of the tonal gradation shown by her skin.

Stark lighting aimed across the front of the subject has created areas of strong shadow. These shadows emphasise the most prominent contours of this part of the body. Note how both of the images here benefit from the use of a black background.

Technical Details
Medium Format SLR Camera with a 210mm telephoto lens and Kodak TMax b&w film.

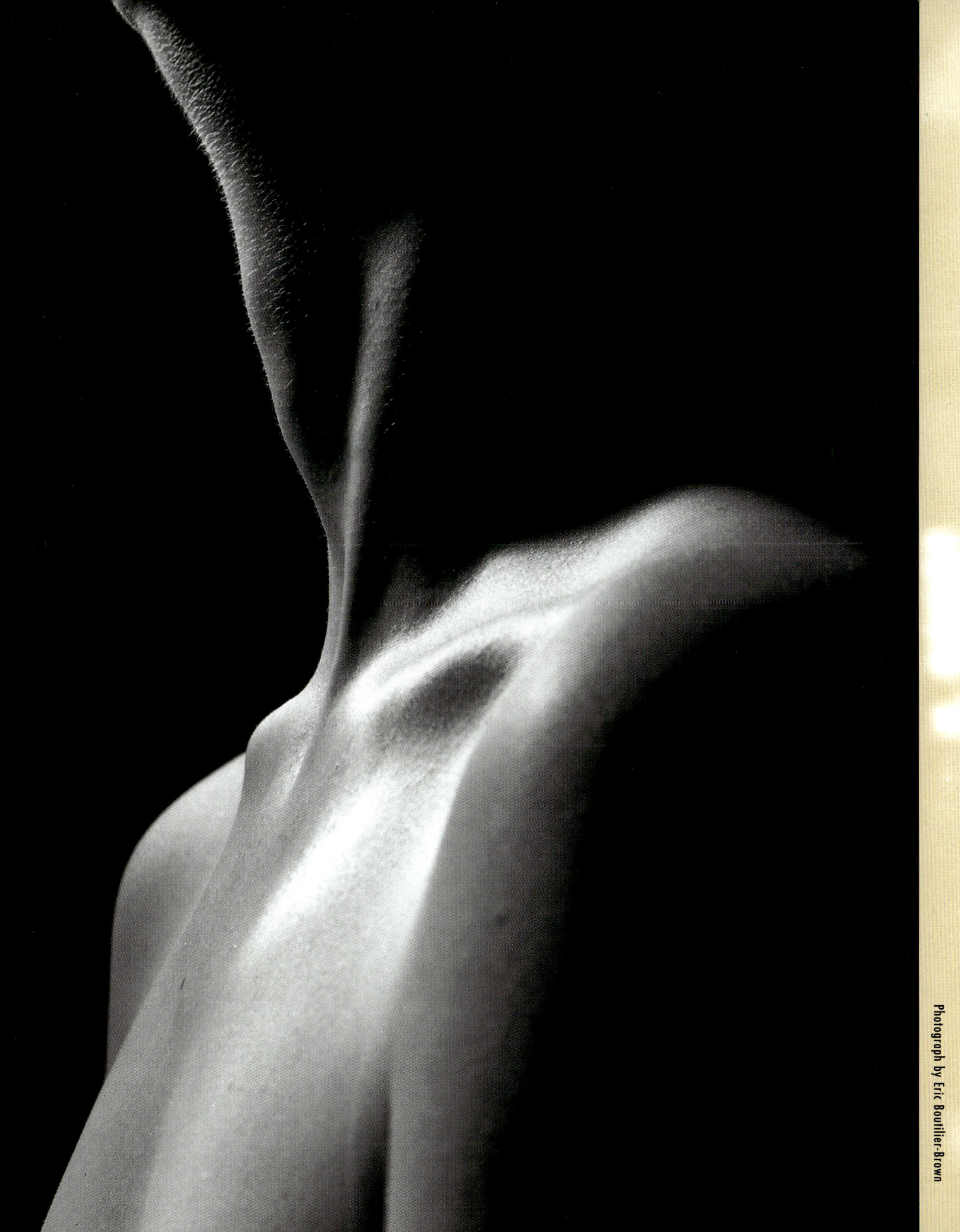

Photograph by Eric Boutilier-Brown

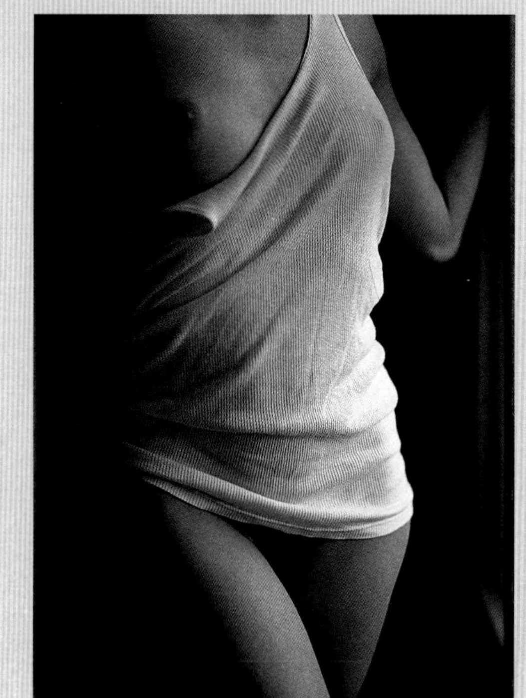

Natural Light

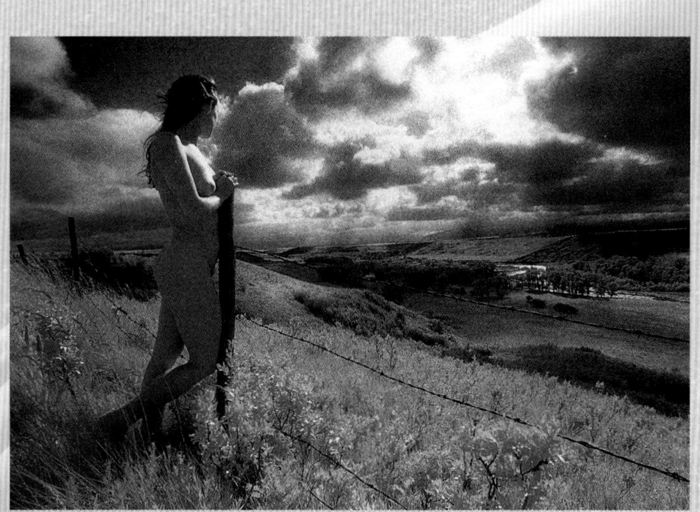

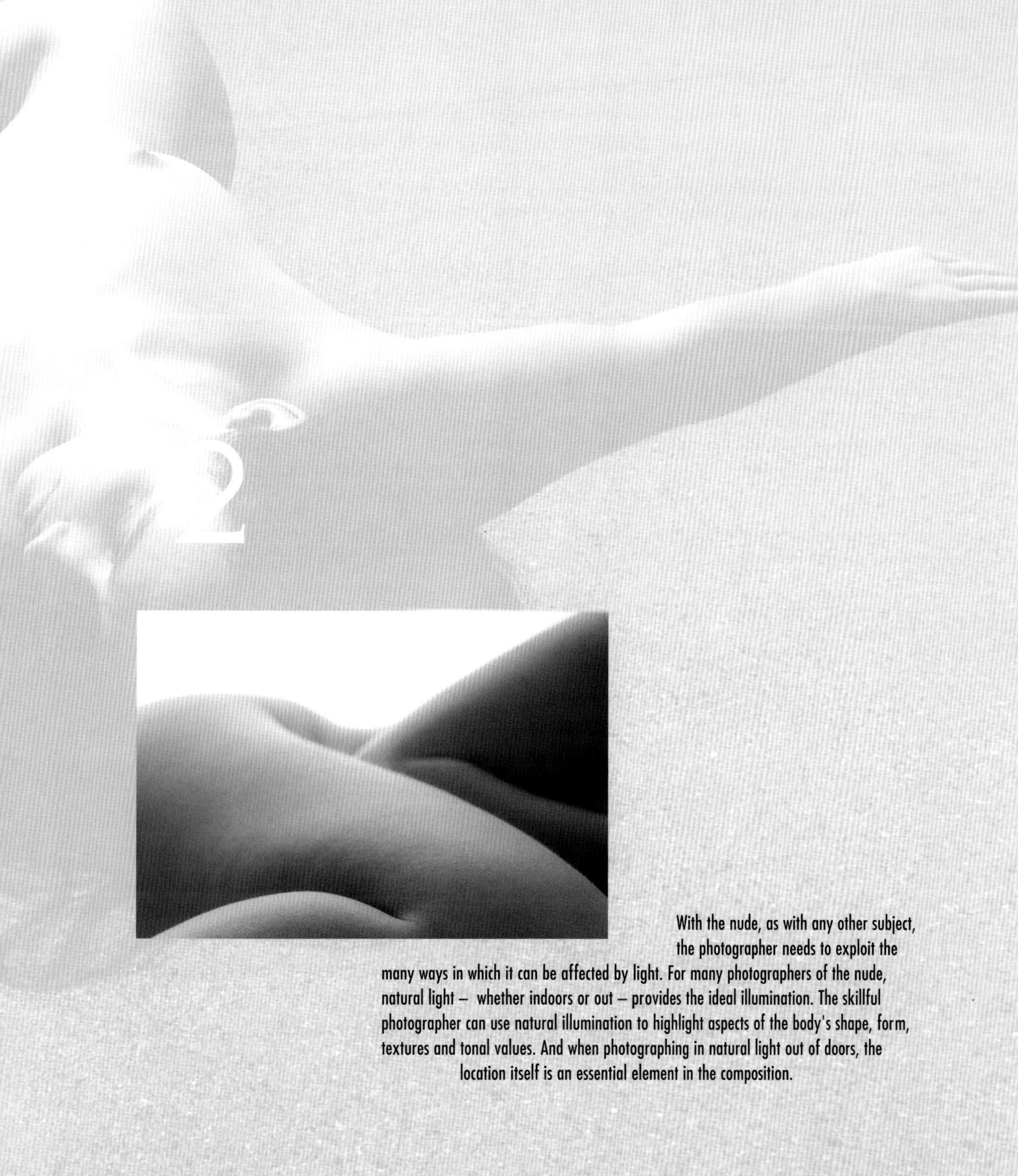

2

With the nude, as with any other subject, the photographer needs to exploit the many ways in which it can be affected by light. For many photographers of the nude, natural light – whether indoors or out – provides the ideal illumination. The skillful photographer can use natural illumination to highlight aspects of the body's shape, form, textures and tonal values. And when photographing in natural light out of doors, the location itself is an essential element in the composition.

Outdoor Light

Shooting outdoors offers a huge variety of locations, backgrounds and lighting conditions, with the sun and the sky acting as a huge natural light source. You do not need sunny days for successful outdoor shots. Bright sunlight creates lively, sparkling images, but can also create harsh shadows and high contrast which are difficult to control. Cloudy, overcast days are often more suitable, as the light is softer and generally kinder to skin tones.

Seeing

The photographer wanted to create a picture in which the human form complemented the contours of the natural landscape. He did not allow the dramatic landscape to overpower the nude figure, nor did he allow the nude to dominate the setting.

Thinking

He also wanted to suggest a sense of narrative. The result could be a scene from a fairy tale or fantasy, and the female figure gives the impression that she belongs in this setting. She looks poised, as if she is just about to move.

Acting

A short telephoto lens allowed him to crop in quite tightly to isolate the part of the scene he wanted to include. It also slightly flattened the perspective of the picture, adding to the brooding sense of narrative.

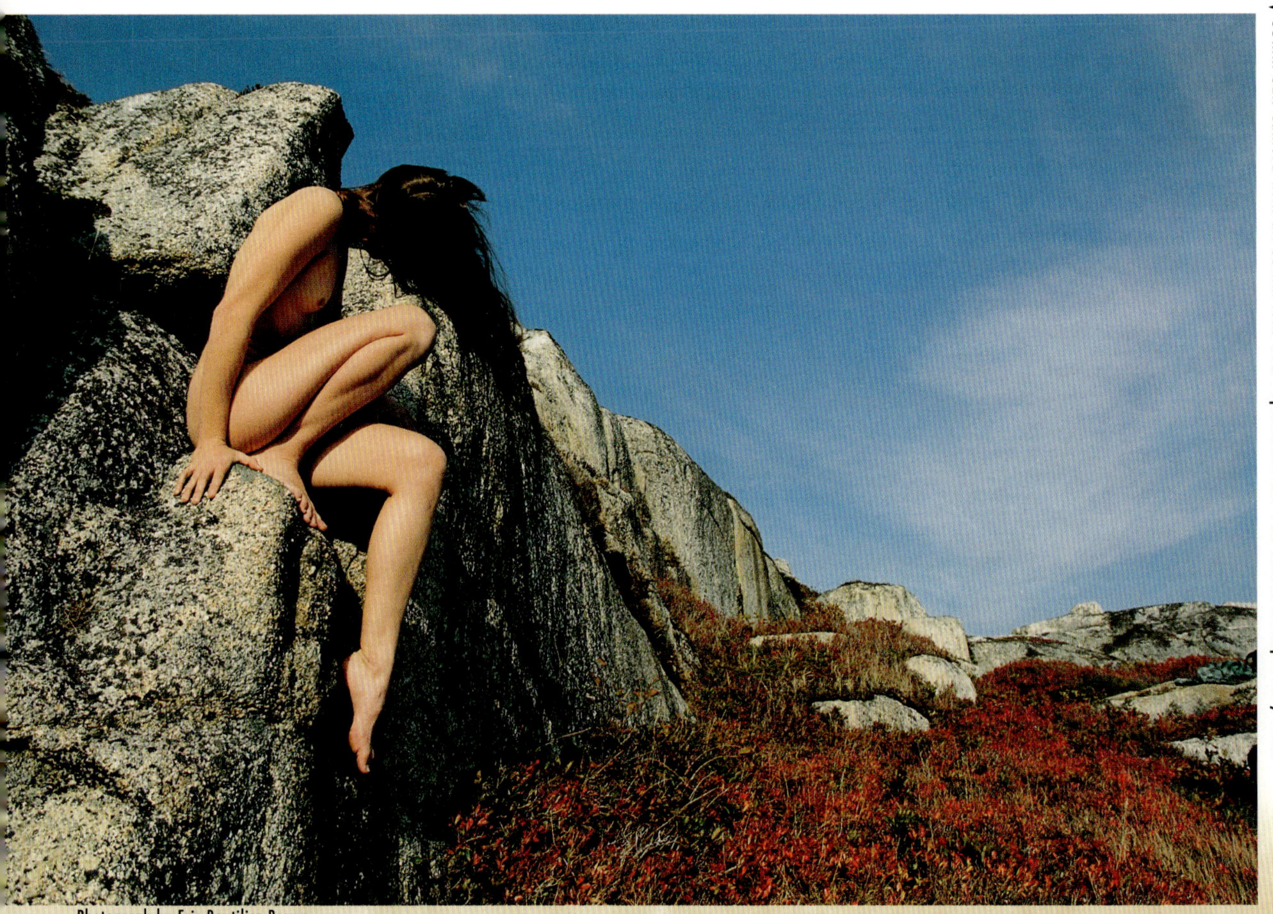

Photograph by Eric Boutilier-Brown

Technical Details

35mm SLR Camera with an 85mm lens and Fujichrome ISO 100 colour transparency film.

Using a tripod enabled a slow shutter speed to be used, and this shows in the way the water has blurred. The medium film format has captured the dappled shadows of the leaves on the woman's body in fine detail.

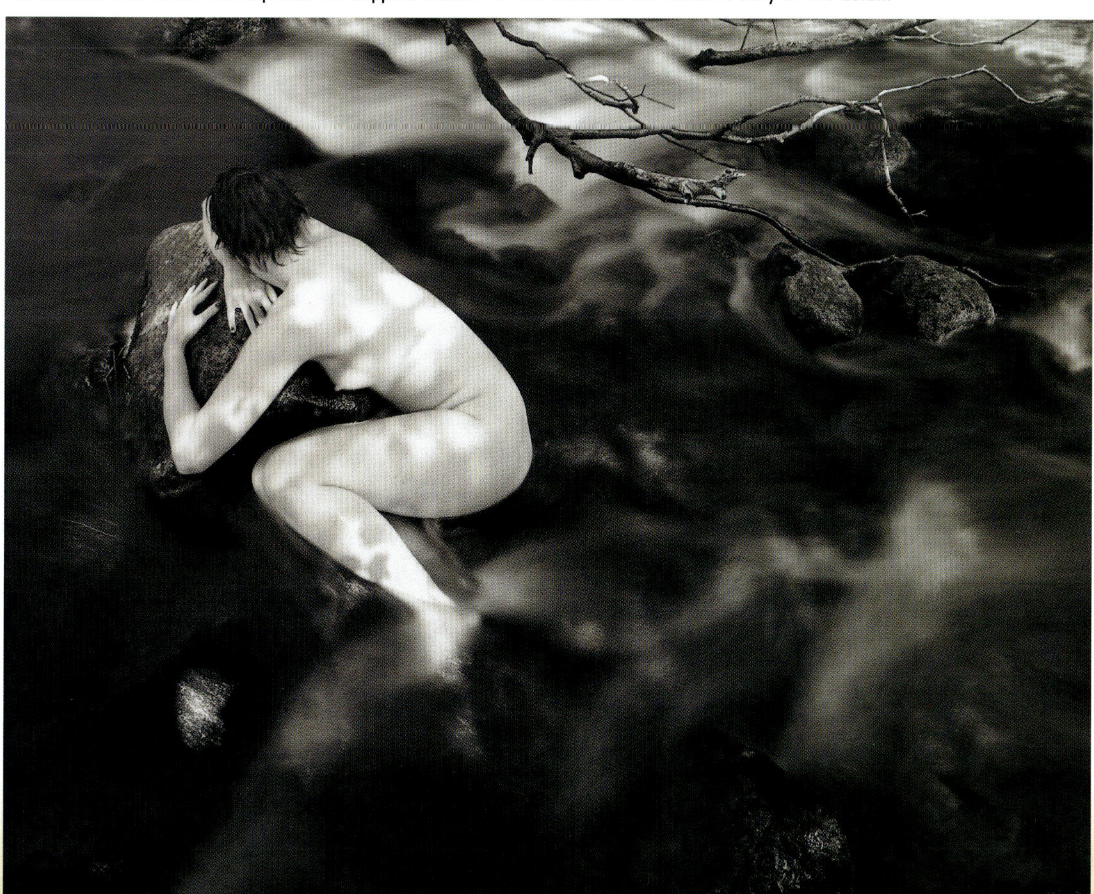

Technical Details

Medium Format SLR Camera with a 90mm lens and Fuji NPS b&w film.

Photograph by Eric Boutilier-Brown

Texture & Tone

Juxtaposing the human figure with the natural landscape gives great scope for semi-abstract shots that rely on textures and shapes for their impact. The texture of human skin photographed together with the textures of natural objects such as rock, sand, wood, foliage or grass makes for a very effective contrast, especially if seen in close-up. Taking a wider view, the shape of the human body can be manipulated to complement, or contrast with, shapes and patterns that occur in nature.

Technical Details

Medium Format Camera with a 50mm lens and Kodak TMax 100 b&w film.

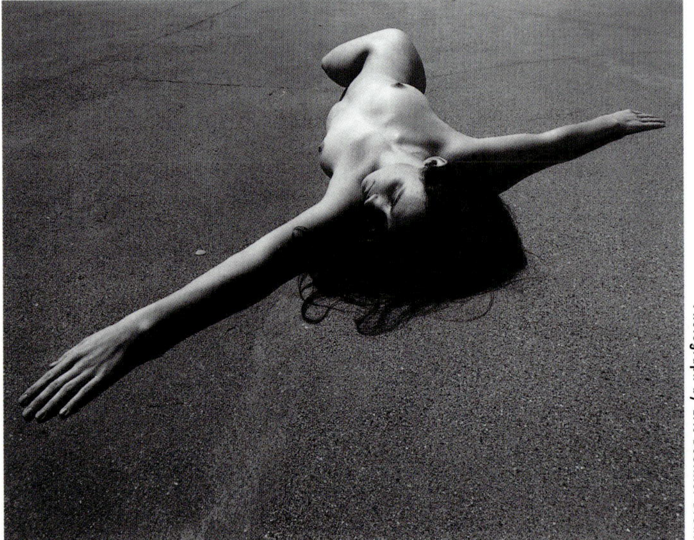

Photograph by Eric Boutilier-Brown

This is a beautifully composed image because of the shape that has been created. The photographer used an extreme wide-angle lens to create a dynamic composition that draws the viewer's eye into the image.

Seeing

The photographer set out to use the texture of the jagged rocks to create a strong contrast with the texture and contours of the living body. He wanted a picture with fine detail that would emphasise the different textures, and so chose to work with a medium format SLR camera.

Thinking

Although a medium format camera gives finely detailed results, using it demands discipline and advanced planning. The locations and framing need to be carefully thought out to get the best results. Setting up takes time so it was important to choose a comfortable position for the model.

Acting

Some SLR cameras don't have built-in exposure meters; instead exposure readings are taken with a separate hand-held light meter. Boutilier-Brown had the model adopt a dramatic pose and used a wide-angle lens to introduce a sense of depth into the picture.

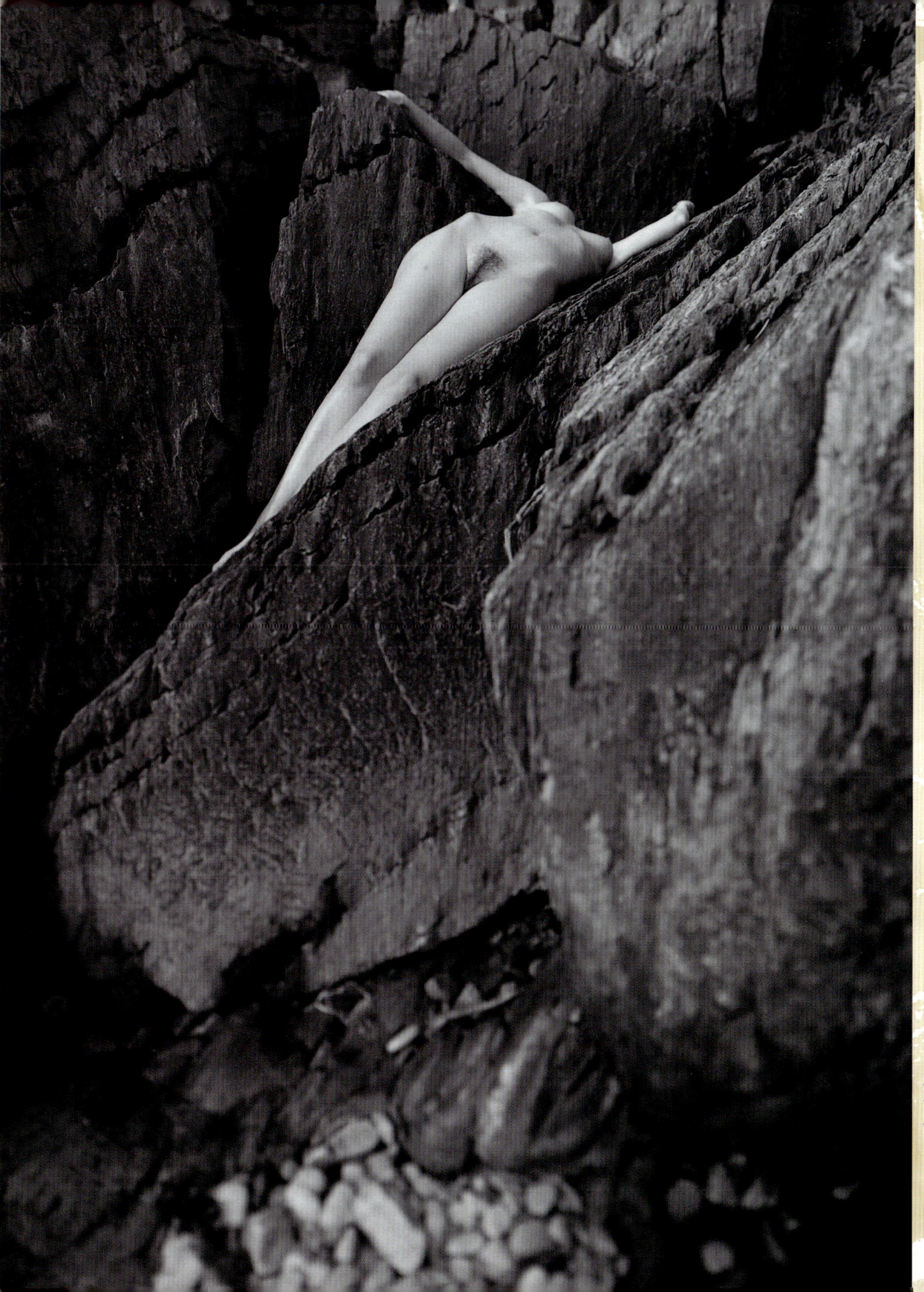

Technical Details

Medium Format SLR Camera with a 50mm lens and Kodak TMax 400 b&w film.

Photograph by Eric Boutilier-Brown

Choosing a Viewpoint

Depending on the viewpoint chosen, the same few elements of a scene can be combined in very different ways. For the photographer, the skill lies in choosing the right lens and the right angle of view to allow the elements to be moulded into the desired image.

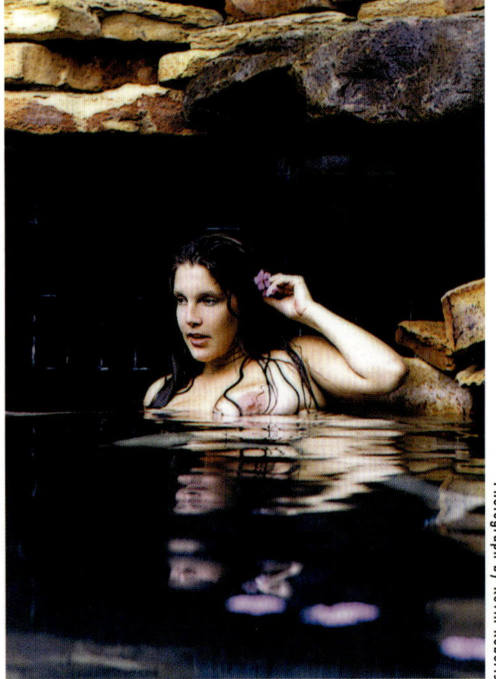

Photograph by Kevin Roberts

The relative smallness of the figure at the centre of the frame and the flattening effect of a long focal-length lens show that this intimate moment was in fact captured from some distance away. Kevin Roberts used a 35mm camera with a long zoom lens set at the telephoto end.

Technical Details

35mm SLR Camera with a 120–600mm zoom lens and Fuji RDP II colour transparency film.

Seeing

The model in this photo is nine months pregnant. The photographer wanted to capture on film what he saw as the compelling beauty of the expectant mother, a combination of inner peace and sensuality.

Thinking

The use of water and flowers was intended to express some of the serenity that the photographer wanted to convey. The colour of the water comes from the reflections of the greenery surrounding the pool. The floating flowers provide complementary points of colour.

Acting

The young woman is sitting on her knees in a pool at a depth where her face just breaks the water. The picture was shot with available light, as flash would have destroyed the effect of the strong overcast lighting. The photographer shot from a high viewpoint and framed the picture so that the subject's face and body form a strong diagonal towards the top left corner of the frame.

Technical Details

35mm SLR Camera with an 85mm lens and Fuji RDP II colour transparency film.

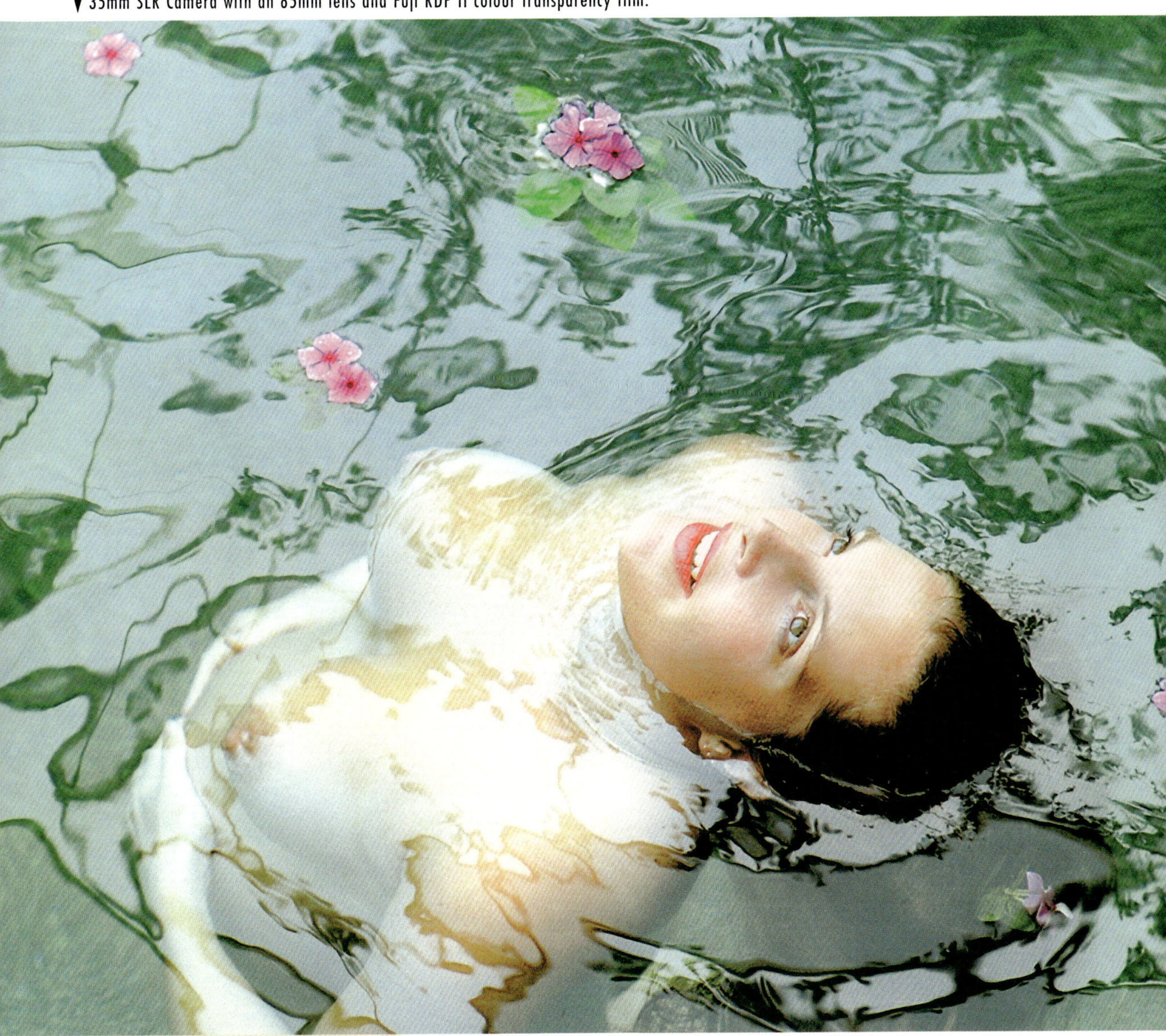

Photograph by Kevin Roberts

Colour & Mood

Differences in the quality of available light greatly affect the mood of the photographic image, particularly when colour film is used. The warm golden tones of a sunset have a very different feeling to the colder, bluer light of morning, for instance. Locations can also affect the result, especially those dominated by a single colour, such as the blue of the sea or an expanse of white/yellow sand. Switching to black and white film concentrates attention on the tonal range of the subject, and highlights shapes and patterns.

Photographs by Kevin Roberts

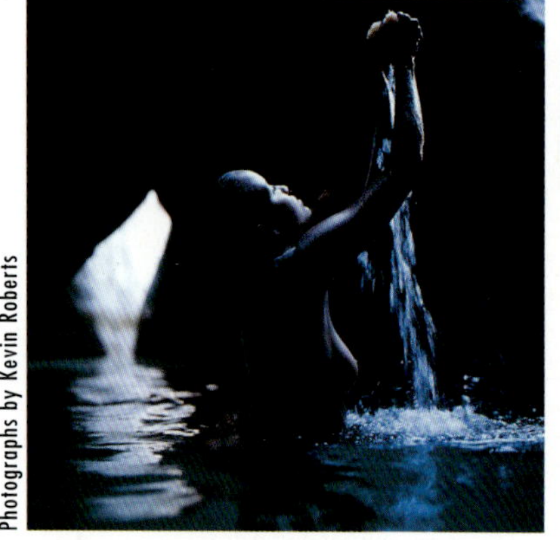

This is not a toned image although it might appear to be so. The mostly blue colouring is an effect of the lighting and the location.

Technical Details
35mm SLR Camera with an 85mm lens and Fujicolour Reala colour print film.

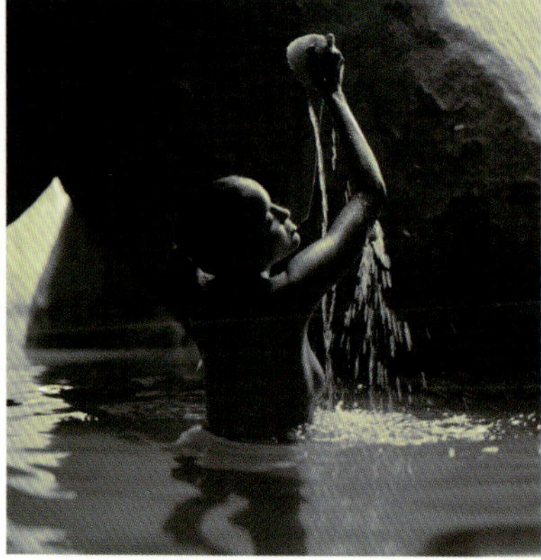

The photographer switched to black and white film for the second shot. Notice how the lack of colour enables the eye to concentrate more on shape, contrast and tonal range.

Technical Details
35mm SLR Camera with an 85mm lens and Kodak TMax 400 b&w film.

Seeing

The sun is actually to the left of the model and behind her, but heavy cloud cover made it little more than a fill light. The main light is provided by the open sky, which acts like a giant reflector.

Thinking

The photographer chose a relatively low camera angle, crouching down on the sand and shooting up at the subject. He also chose to include an expanse of beach and sea as the background. Shooting a standing figure from such a low viewpoint makes it appear more dynamic.

Acting

As it was approaching dusk on an overcast day and the film was ISO 100, the photographer had to use a slow shutter speed. He was also obliged to use a large aperture, which meant a very limited depth of field. Once he had printed the picture, he toned it a warm sepia colour in the darkroom.

Technical Details

35mm SLR Camera with an 85mm lens and Kodak TMax 100 b&w film.

Photograph by Kevin Roberts

Window Light

Daylight falling naturally through a window is one of the most commonly used – and most appealing – forms of illumination for photographers of the nude. So appealing is it, in fact, that much artificial lighting equipment is designed to reproduce its effect. It requires little more equipment than is normally used for straightforward outdoor shots, although a reflector is often useful to even out shadow areas by throwing light back on to the subject.

Seeing

Sally Russ hadn't planned this image beforehand but saw the potential for it in the course of a shooting session. The window light provided the inspiration, and Russ chose to use it in a way that emphasised the texture of the model's skin and that of the garment she was wearing. The tight crop concentrated attention on shape and form.

Thinking

The main light source was natural daylight coming in through a window. A white covered bed nearby reflected some of the incoming daylight back into the dark areas.

Acting

Although the photographer had a fast film loaded in her camera, the exposure still required a shutter speed of 1/60 sec. The resulting image was a straight print without any dodging or burning-in.

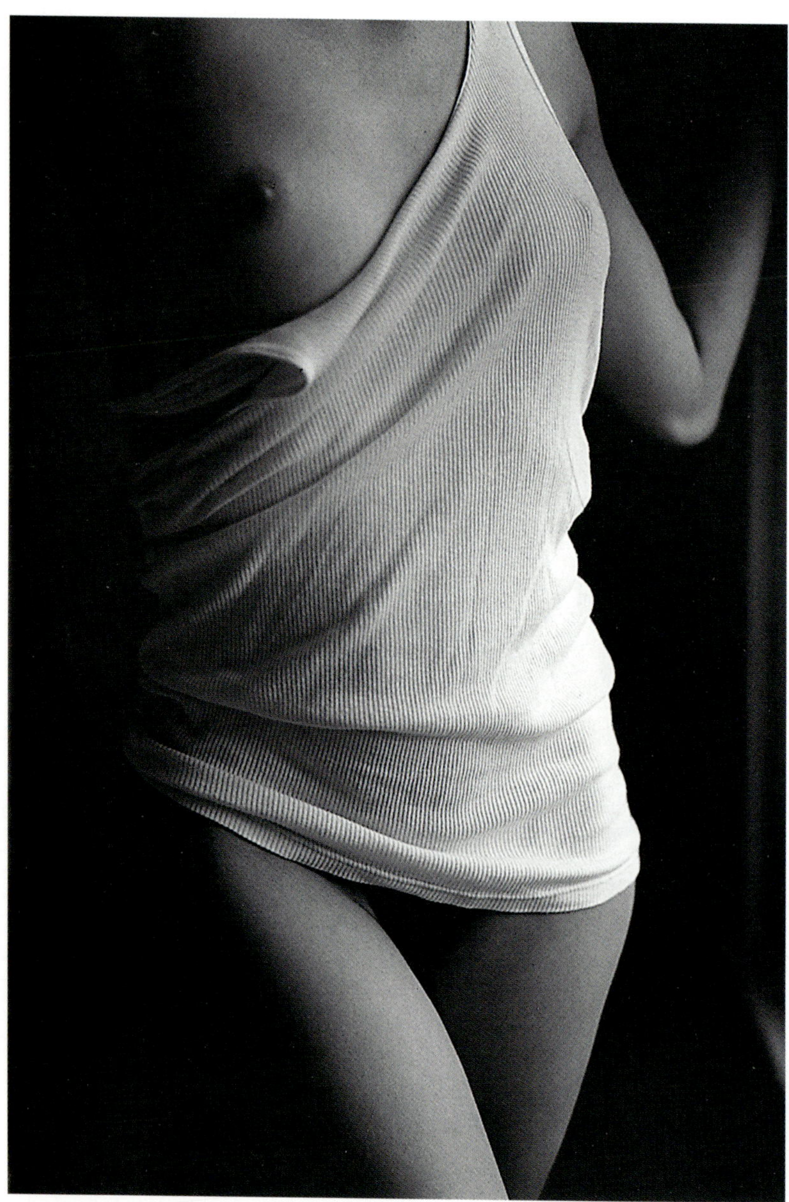

Photograph by Sally Russ

Technical Details

35mm SLR Camera with an 85mm lens and Kodak Tri-X ISO 400 b&w film.

The brightness of the light coming from the window caused the highlight areas to be very bright while plunging the area behind the girl into deep shadow. The photographer concentrated attention on the girl's hair and the flimsy white material she was draped in while deliberately obscuring her face in order to create an ethereal, other-worldly impression.

Technical Details

35mm SLR Camera with a 28–85mm lens and Kodak TMax 400 b&w film.

Photograph by Sally Russ

Detailed Lighting

Natural light provides soft, even illumination for detail shots of the human body, picking out contours and skin textures in a way that concentrates the viewer's attention on shape and form. It can be replicated in the studio by using tools such as a softbox. Shots of this type more often than not have an abstract quality to them.

Technical Details
Medium Format Camera with a 210mm telephoto lens and Kodak TMax 100 b&w film.

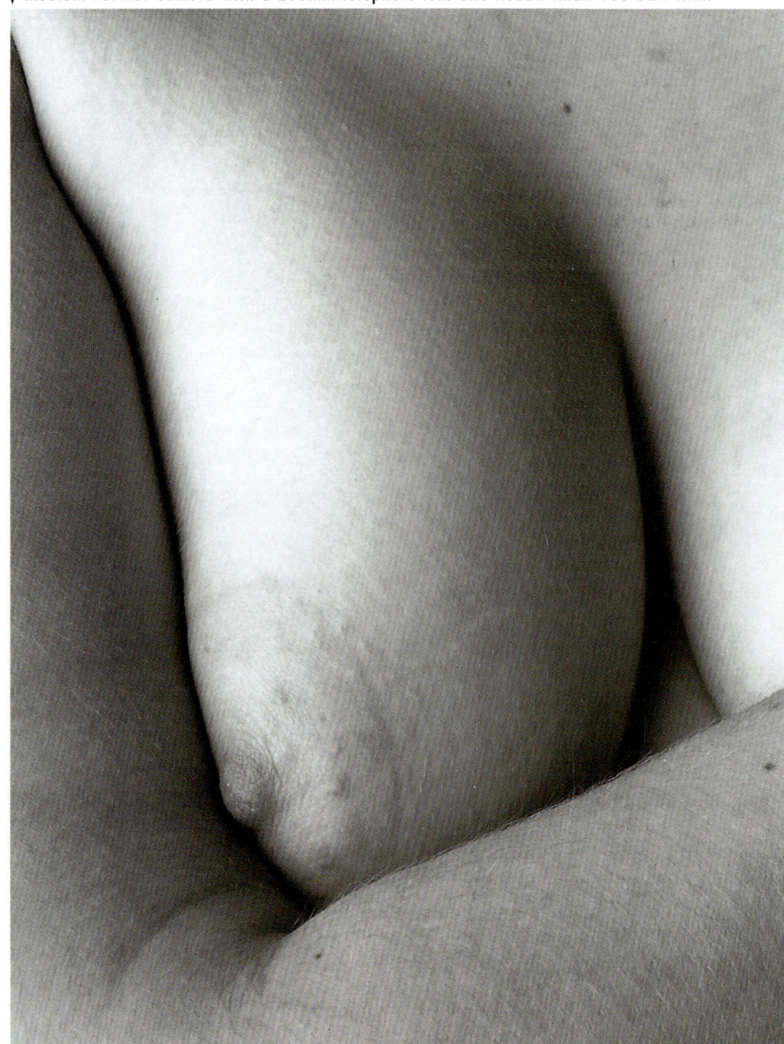

Photograph by Eric Boutilier-Brown

Seeing

The photographer wanted to use the contours of the female form to create an abstract image that relied on a few simple lines for its impact. At the same time the subject is still recognisably part of the human body.

Thinking

The powerful, even illumination from a softbox enhances the texture and form. Although an abstract image, this part of the breast and the inner elbow form a strong, simple composition that is immediately recognisable. The photographer lit the image to emphasise the contours of the model's body, so that some areas appeared as bright highlights while others, by contrast, were thrown into shadow.

Acting

The photographer had to balance the exposure carefully for the strong lighting so that the bright areas didn't appear overexposed and the shadow areas weren't too dark. He used a softbox to give powerful, even illumination which brought out the texture of the model's skin.

Technical Details
35mm SLR Camera with an 85mm lens and Fuji Sensia colour transparency film.

Eric Boutilier-Brown used soft, diffuse lighting to illuminate this abstract torso shot and a short telephoto lens to crop in close. The flowing lines of the background fabric echo the curves of the model's body.

Photograph by Eric Boutilier-Brown

Indoor Daylight

You do not need to be out of doors to make use of natural daylight. Windows and open doors can be used as the source of illumination even when the location is the interior of a building. Strong directional sunlight works best in this situation, although careful placing of the model is necessary and reflectors may be needed to even out harsh shadows. Shadows, however, can be used to positive effect, creating patterns across the model's body and the interior of the room.

Technical Details

Medium Format Camera with a 150mm lens and Ilford HP5 ISO 400 b&w film.

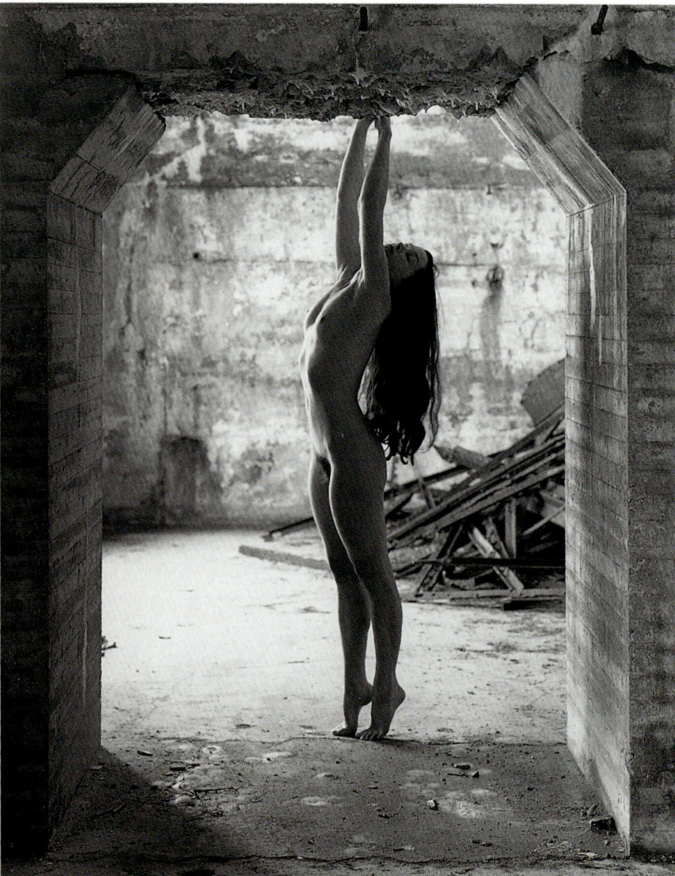

Photograph by Eric Boutilier-Brown

The photographer carefully chose the time of day so that the interior of the room was illuminated by strong sunlight coming through an open doorway. This allowed him to expose for the highlights on the model's body without turning her into a semi-silhouette. The brick archway formed a natural frame for the subject.

Seeing

This image relies totally on available light that has been controlled and used in a most effective way. The photographer scouted the location beforehand and visualised his picture. He knew it would work on a sunny day when the sunlight was falling at the right angle to illuminate the interior of the room.

Thinking

The large window, besides being the main source of illumination for the scene, also forms a frame for the subject. The photographer paid close attention to the classic compositional device of the rule of thirds, using the window to split the frame into three roughly equal vertical sections and placing the model at an intersection of thirds.

Acting

The photographer treated the daylight entering the room like the illumination from a giant lamp. He used a piece of card and a white wall as a large reflector, bouncing light back towards the model. Without this she would probably have appeared as a semi-silhouette.

Photograph by Eric Boutilier-Brown

Technical Details

Medium Format Camera with a 120mm lens and Kodak TMax 400 b&w film.

Nude & Landscape

Placing a nude figure within a landscape is a device which has painterly traditions dating back to classical times. It requires a feeling for nude photography together with an understanding of the compositional rules of landscapes. If it is done well, the nude figure will look at ease within the landscape, and not at all awkward or out of place. A dramatic composition can suggest a sense of narrative, as if the picture has a story to tell.

Seeing

The sweeping landscape and the towering cloud formations formed a perfect backdrop for the nude figure. Although the textures of the landscape are relatively soft, the photographer made a point of including the jagged barbed wire fence, which introduces a strongly contrasting texture into the image.

Thinking

Great care was taken over composition, with the photographer using an ultra wide-angle lens to include a very wide area of the scene in front of him in the shot. He positioned the woman at the intersection of thirds. While she is the focal point the panorama on the right forms a perfect balance.

Acting

The photographer used black and white Infrared for the shot. He enhanced the effect by using a red filter, which has also darkened the colour of the sky and made the clouds stand out more distinctly.

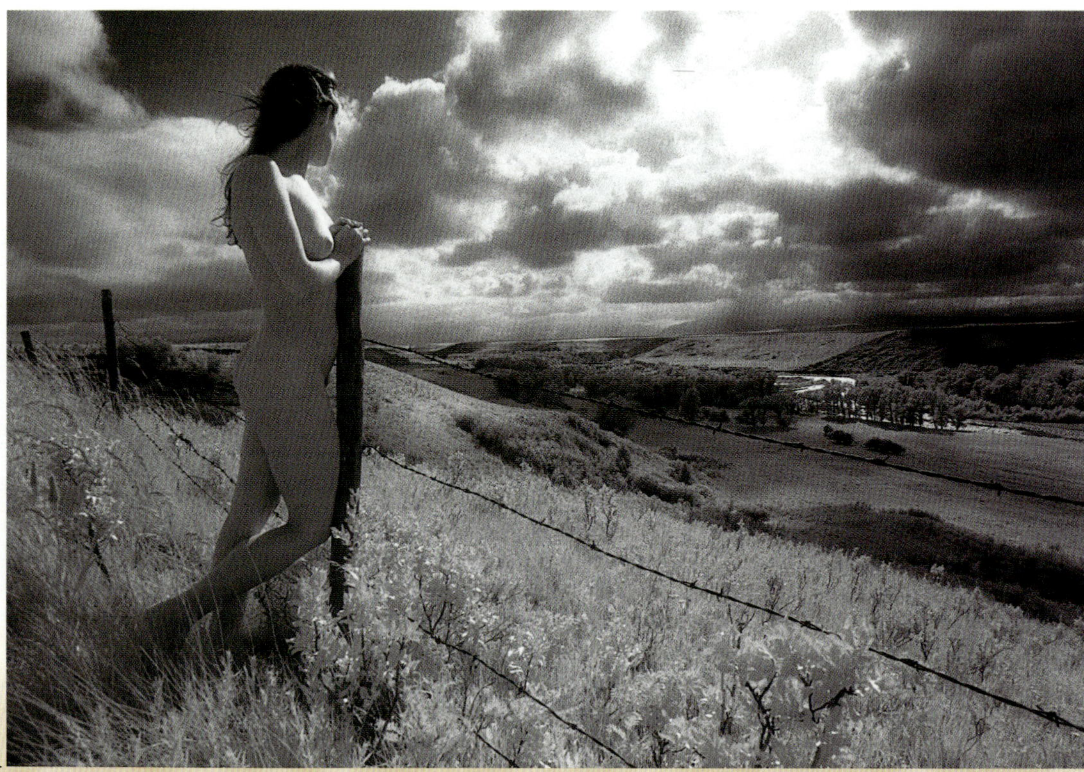

Technical Details
35mm SLR Camera with a 20mm lens and Kodak Infrared b&w film.

Photograph by Eric Bouttlier-Brown

Photograph by Eric Boutillier-Brown

The photographer composed this image so that the contours of the woman's body echoed the soft ripples of the sand dunes and the cloud formations in the sky. The glow on the woman's skin is a typical characteristic of black and white infrared film. A red filter enhanced the contrast.

Technical Details

Medium Format Camera with a 50mm lens and Kodak TMax 400 b&w film.

Differential Focus

Focusing is one of the simplest, yet most effective, compositional devices. By concentrating attention on a particular part of the body and allowing the rest of the composition to fall out of focus, an illusion of depth can be created within the image. Natural daylight is usually strong enough to allow the full range of lens apertures to be exploited in controlling depth of field.

Seeing

Eric Boutilier-Brown wanted to create a feeling of depth by highlighting one element of the image while allowing the others to recede into the background. He achieved this by using differential focus, which is essentially a way of creating selective soft focus through shallow depth of field. A small part of the image appears in sharp focus while the rest is blurred and indistinct.

Thinking

The photographer chose the model's mouth and chin for the areas of sharper focus. He used a short telephoto lens, which allowed him to crop in closely on the part of the subject he wanted to include in the frame.

Acting

By using the widest aperture on his lens the photographer was able to make the background areas appear out of focus. He made the effect all the more striking by composing the image so that the sharp areas were off-centre, to one side. He did this by first focusing on the model's mouth and then holding that focus while he re-framed the image.

Technical Details

35mm SLR Camera with a 100mm lens and Fujichrome 400 colour transparency film.

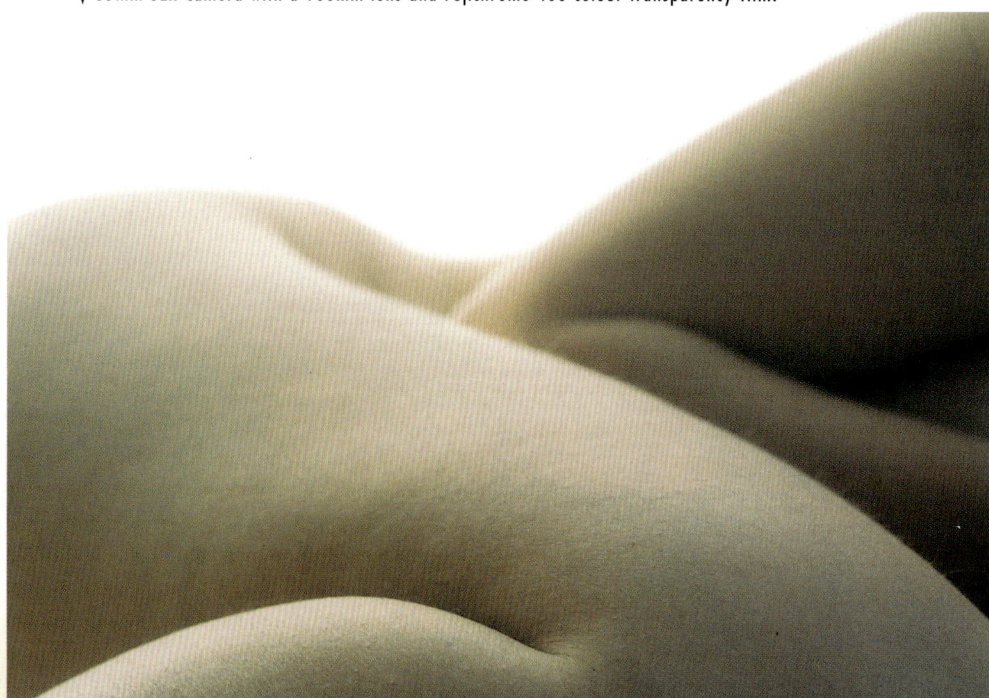

Photograph by Eric Boutilier-Brown

The photographer used differential focus to create this 'body landscape'. The foreground is the only sharp area, while the wide aperture has thrown the rest of the body out of focus. The areas of receding sharpness increase the effect of distance and perspective in the shot.

Photograph by Eric Boutilier-Brown

Technical Details

▼35mm SLR Camera with an 85mm lens and Fujichrome 400 colour transparency film.

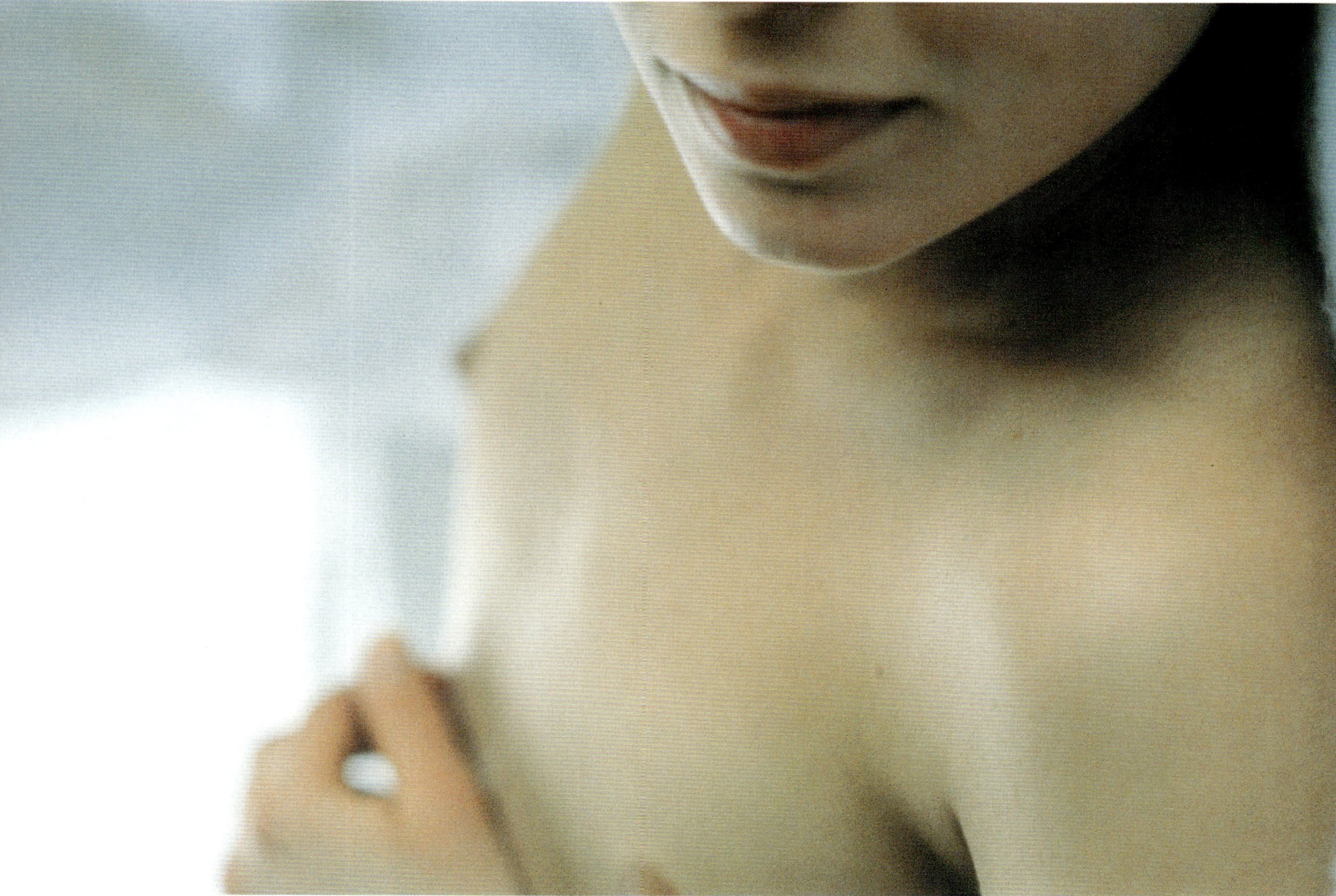

Striking a Pose

Be bold! Asking your model to strike a pose can add impact and drama to the photograph. The pose can suggest a particular activity or a period of history that will have resonance for the viewer of the photograph. Props and backgrounds can be used to enhance the mood that is being created. Alternatively, a pose can simply be an arrangement of the model's limbs or body that creates a shape or pattern and gives geometric form to the image.

Seeing

Pascal Baetens created this striking image out of virtually nothing. All he had to work with was an empty space with a single prop, the raised platform. However, the strong natural daylight filtering into the space gave him the idea for the picture.

Thinking

Using the platform as a pedestal, he asked the model to adopt a statue-like pose. Her raised and open arms suggest the idea that she is involved in some kind of mystical or religious ritual. The air of mystery is enhanced by the strong sidelighting, which suggests the light of the rising or setting sun.

Acting

Baetens positioned the model carefully so that the sunlight caught her body the way he wanted it. He then exposed for the highlights, which had the effect of rendering the model's body in sharp detail but throwing the background area behind her into deep shadow.

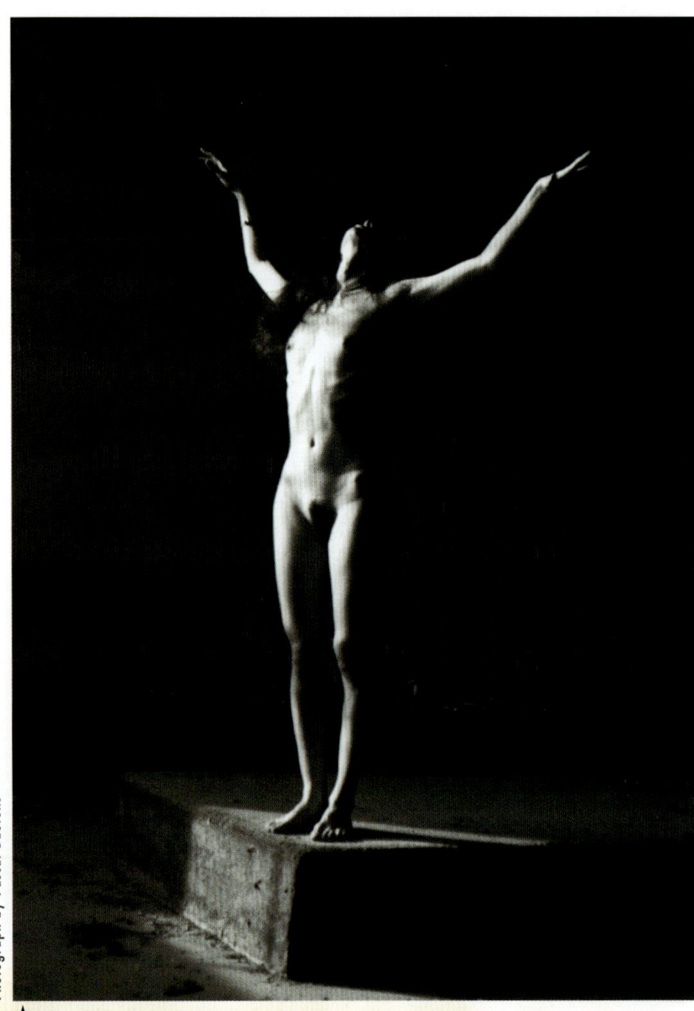

Photograph by Pascal Baetens

Technical Details

35mm SLR Camera with a 35–70mm zoom lens and Kodak TMax 400 b&w film.

The photographer asked the model to pose so that her limbs formed this graphic geometric pattern, which he captured by shooting from a dizzying overhead viewpoint.

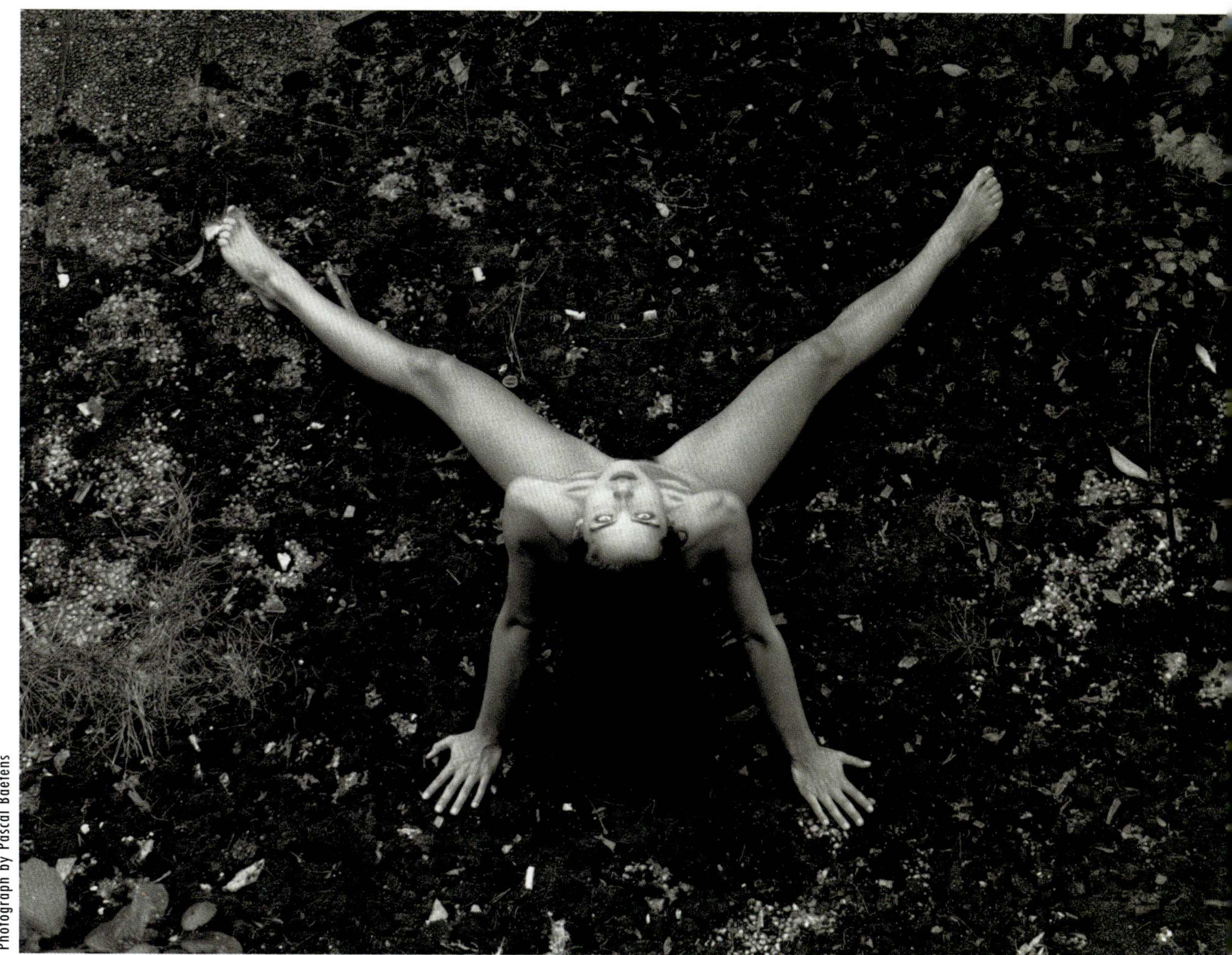

Photograph by Pascal Baetens

Technical Details

35mm SLR Camera with a 28–85mm zoom lens and Kodak TMax 100 b&w film.

Shadow & Form

Shadows can be used to emphasise the shape and form of the body. Areas obscured by deep shadow are if anything more suggestive than areas that are clearly illuminated. This allows the photographer to make subtle use of light and dark areas to impart a deliberate sense of mood.

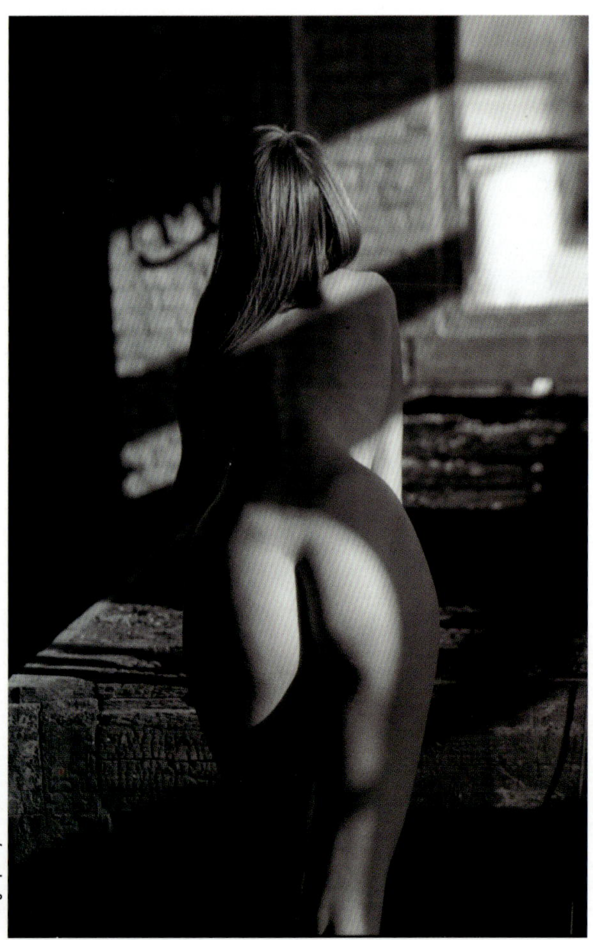

Photograph by Pascal Baetans

Strong shadows are often best left alone. In this image the extreme contrast between light and dark caused by the heavy shadows emphasises shape and form in an almost 3-D way.

Technical Details

35mm SLR Camera with a 28–85mm zoom lens and Kodak TMax b&w film.

Seeing

Heavy shadow areas are usually considered a problem to be corrected by reflectors or flash. In this image, however, Pascal Baetens used them to advantage. He made deliberate use of strong natural light to emphasise the shape and form of his subject's body.

Thinking

The direct noon sunlight was coming through a ceiling window, from above, behind and slightly to the left of the model. The photographer positioned her so that her breasts and hip were highlighted by the slanting sunlight while her face was obscured by deep shadow.

Acting

Very little exposure adjustment was required. The photographer took a straight exposure reading from the bright areas, which automatically rendered the shadow areas dark.

Rule of Thumb

Shadow areas can be eliminated or reduced by the use of reflectors or flash. In situations that require a reduction in shadow areas, and where neither a reflector nor a flash is immediately available, the photographer will need to improvise. A piece of white card, pages from a newspaper, even a pale-coloured item of clothing, suitably positioned, can provide a moderate amount of reflectance.

Technical Details

35mm SLR Camera with a 35–70mm zoom lens and Kodak TMax 400 b&w film.

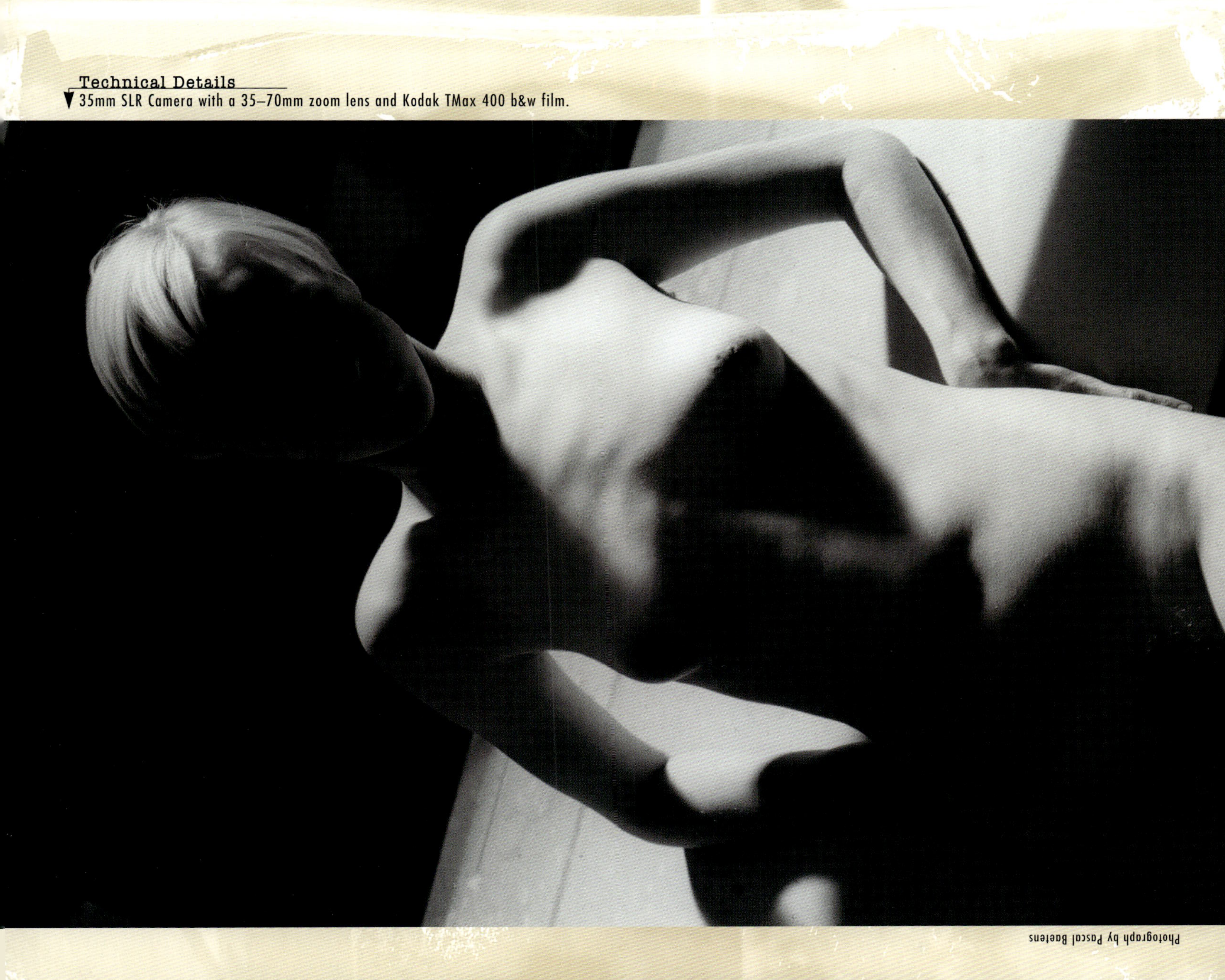

Photograph by Pascal Baetens

Shadow & Form

Seeing

Pascal Baetens used the drama of sunlight and shadow as an integral part of this composition. The main area of interest is the brightly lit model in the foreground, but the light slanting through the grilled windows of the old industrial building also create plenty of background interest.

Thinking

The photographer shot from a low position. This made the girl's figure appear a more dominant part of the composition. It has also given emphasis to the shadows on the floor area.

Acting

The photographer exposed for the strong sidelighting on the model's body and the brick wall in the foreground. This threw the interior of the building into deep shadow, although this was broken up by the light coming from the windows in the far wall. The final result is a complex interplay of light, shadow and form.

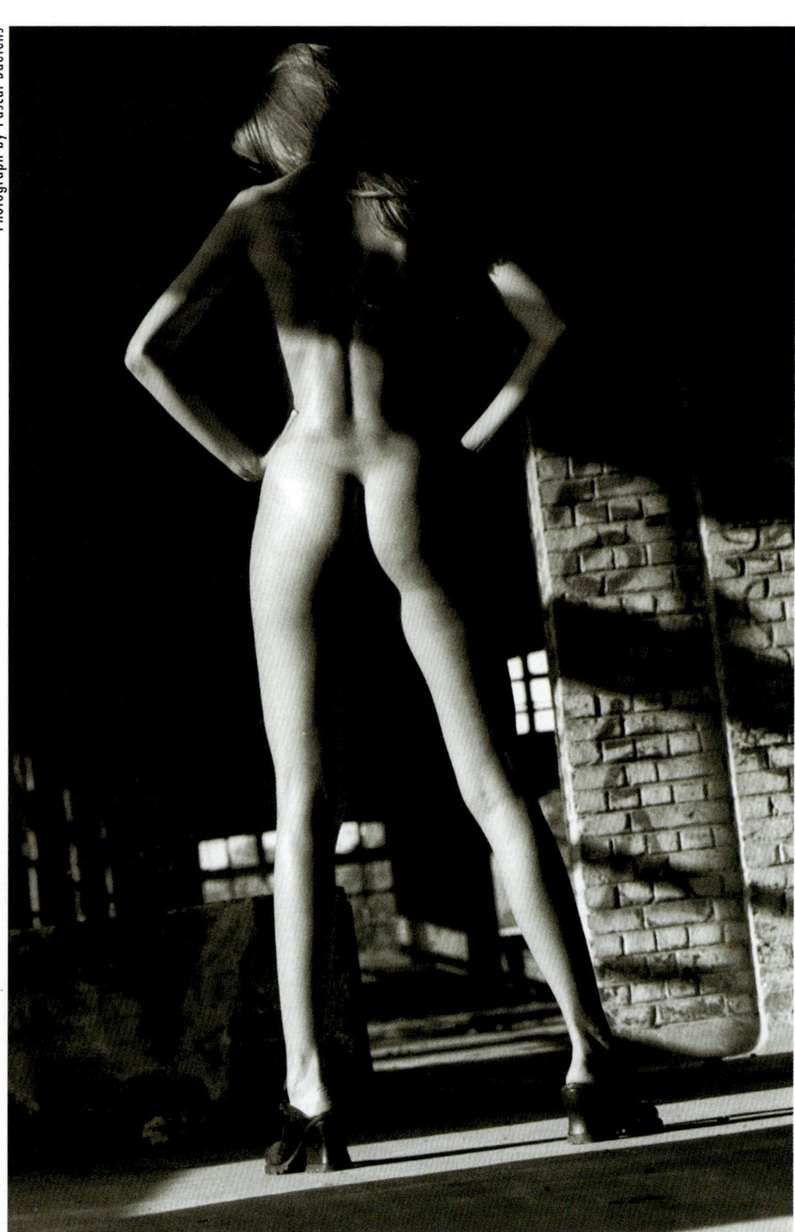

Photograph by Pascal Baetens

Technical Details

35mm SLR Camera with a 35–70mm zoom lens and Kodak TMax 400 b&w film.

Rene de Carufel used strong sidelighting at a very narrow angle to the woman's body to throw her sharply defined shadow on to the wall. The fact that her face is hidden concentrates attention on the curves of her body. These form a striking contrast with the rigid rectangular shapes of the bricks and the shadow of the window frame.

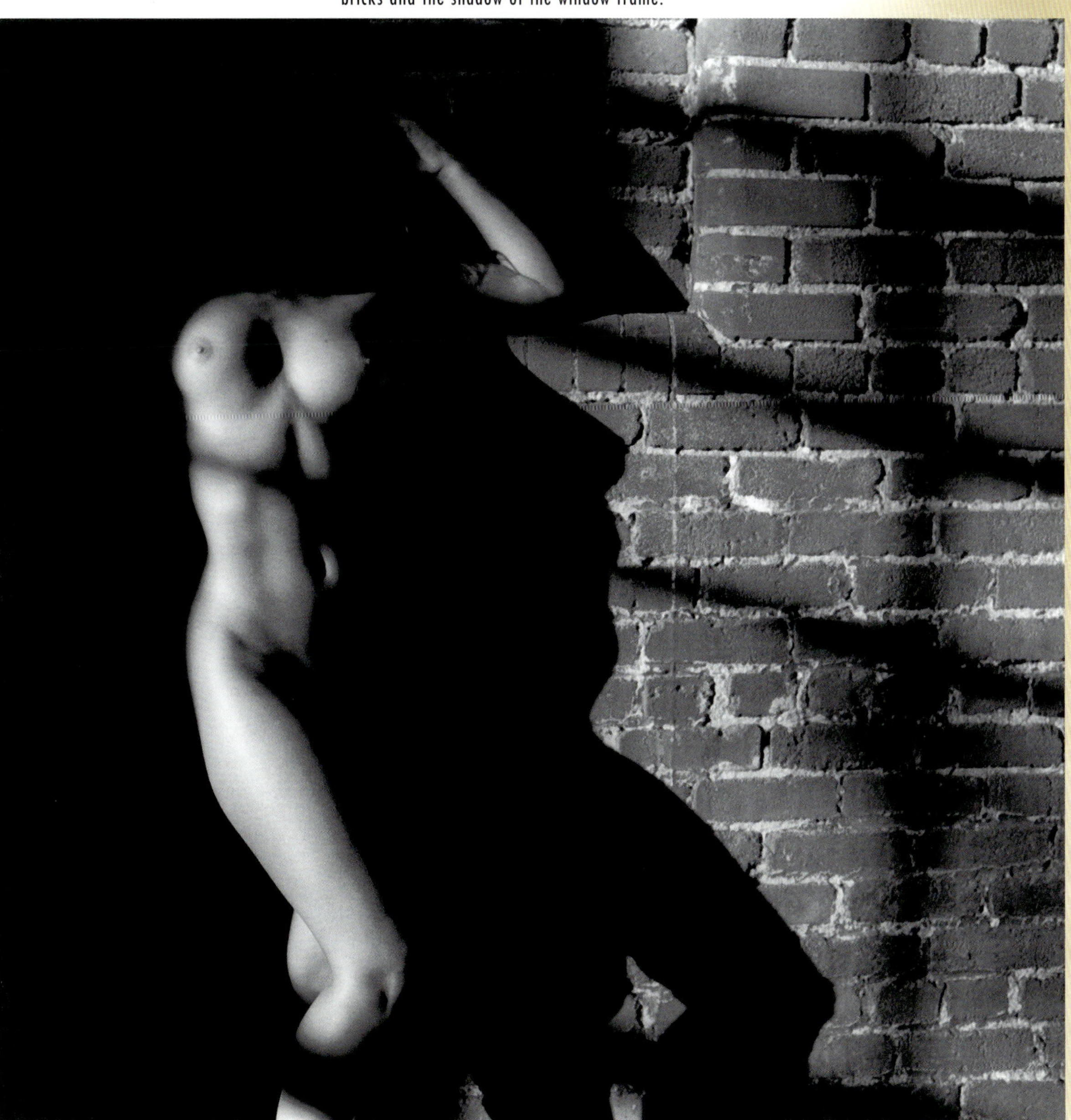

Photograph by Rene de Carufel

Technical Details

Medium Format Camera with a 150mm telephoto lens and Ilford HP5 b&w film.

Flash & Effects

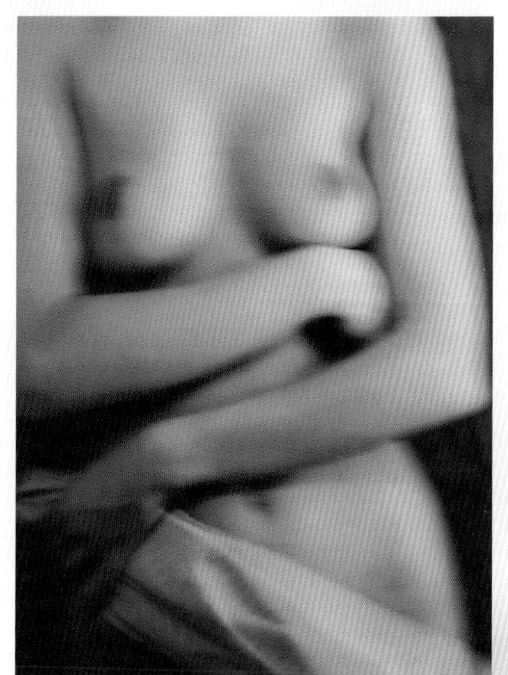

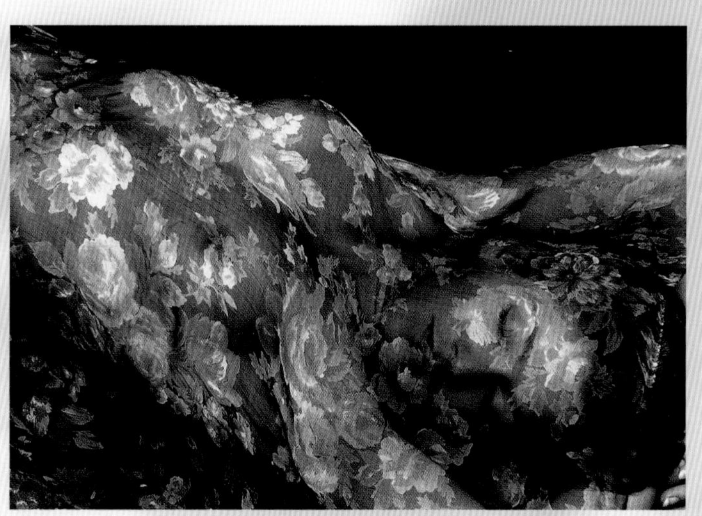

7

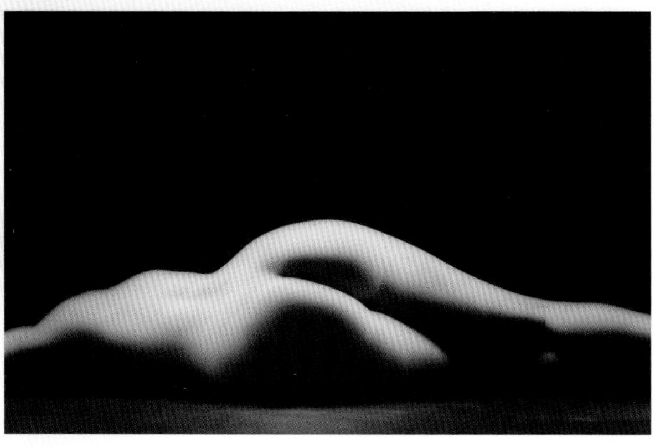

Flash provides the photographer of the nude with ultimate control over lighting. Many photographers approach the lighting of the nude as they would a still life, deciding where to place the shadows in the composition for maximum effect. Such control over lighting makes it easier for the photographer to use lighting effects to create a particular atmosphere, and to evoke an emotional response from the viewer.

Soft Focus

Soft focus is an atmospheric effect that is well suited to nude subjects. It can be achieved indoors or out, either through the use of special filters or by manipulating the characteristics of camera and lens.

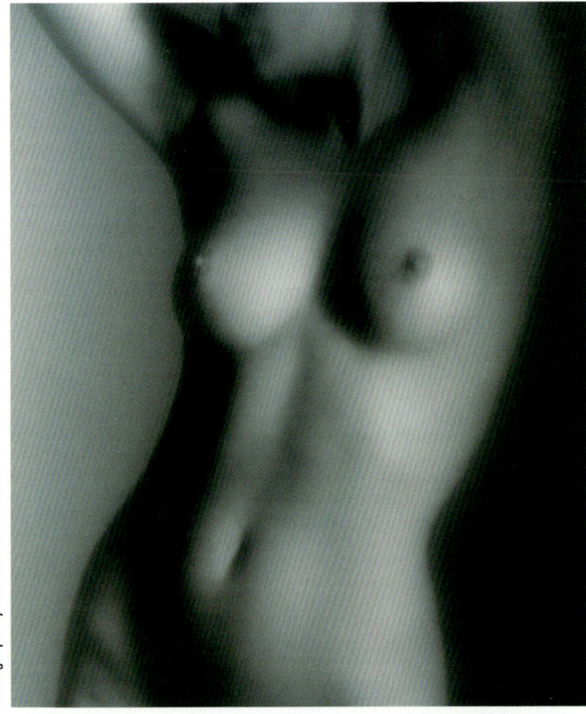

Photograph by Eric Boutilier-Brown

The photographer used a conventional soft-focus filter effect. These filters come in different strengths depending on whether an extreme or a subtle soft-focus effect is required. They are ideally suited to portraiture.

Seeing

Eric Boutilier-Brown wanted to create a selective soft-focus effect that would keep the model's face sharp while throwing the rest of her body out of focus. He kept the lines of the composition clean and simple to focus attention on the face, and so chose a plain back background that made the subject stand out.

Thinking

He achieved this effect by using the perspective control lens which gets rid of converging verticals – the effect that makes the top of an object (photographed from close up) seem to taper to a point.

Acting

He tilted the camera to ensure that only the subject's face was in sharp focus, while the rest of her body was out of focus. By doing this it centres the focus of attention on to the model's face.

Rule of Thumb

A photographer has an advantage over a painter when asking a model to strike a pose that may be physically difficult to maintain. A painter's model may need to hold a pose for several minutes. A photograph, on the other hand, takes just a fraction of a second. The photographer's model will therefore experience less discomfort because the instant when the photograph is taken, and therefore also the pose, is short-lived.

Technical Details (▲)

35mm SLR Camera with a 28–70mm zoom lens and Fujichrome 400 colour transparency film.

Technical Details (►)

Medium Format SLR Camera with a 210mm lens and Kodak TMax 100 b&w film.

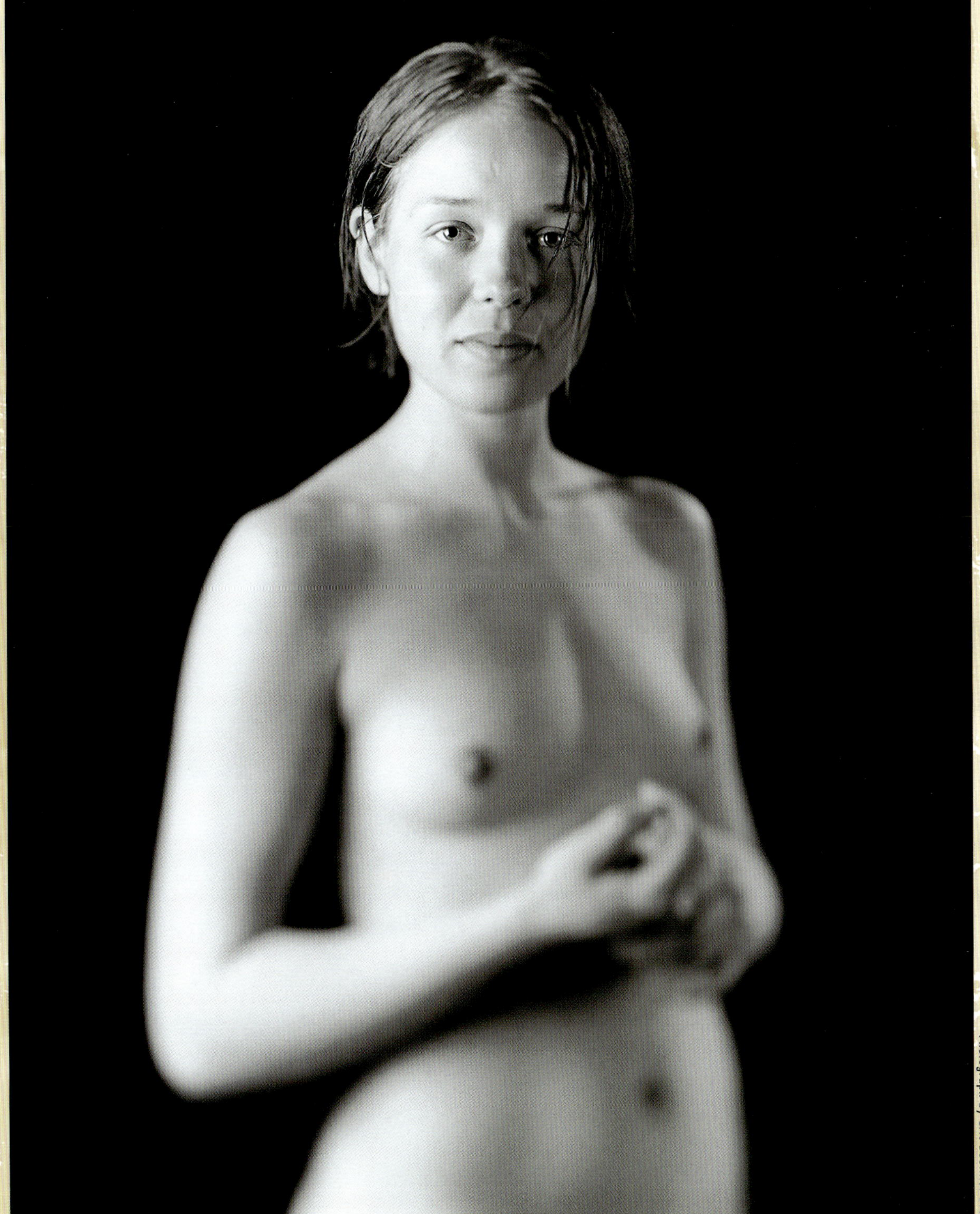

Photograph by Eric Boutilier-Brown

The Torso

Portraying the human torso in isolation is a tradition that dates back to the sculpture of classical antiquity. For the photographer of nudes it remains a striking compositional device. Careful positioning of lighting can be used to emphasise the statuesque comparison.

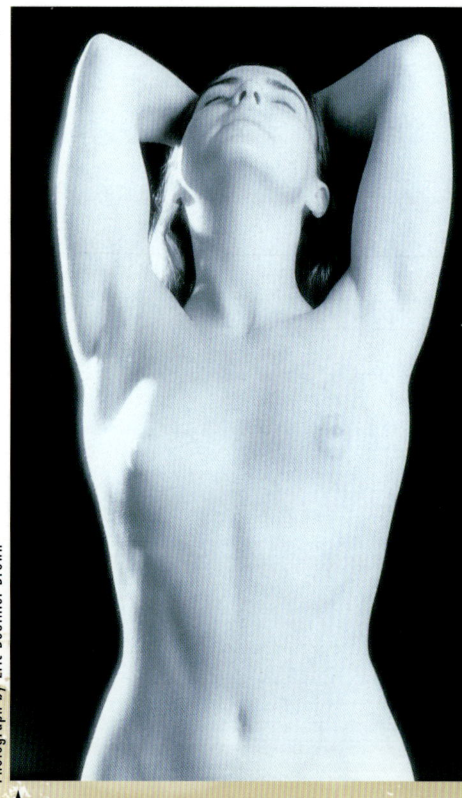

Photograph by Eric Boutilier-Brown

Technical Details
35mm SLR Camera with an 85mm telephoto lens and Kodak High Speed Infrared b&w film.

Seeing

The photographer used a combination of black and white infrared film and strong studio lighting to create this image. Infrared film creates a glowing effect as it is sensitive to heat waves as well as to the light waves that are normally recorded by photographic film. The result is eerie but distinctive.

Thinking

Once the model had adopted her statuesque pose, the photographer cropped in close with a short telephoto 85mm lens, which is most often used for portraiture. He posed and lit her in such a way that the background appeared pure black, forming a kind of frame within a frame for the eerily lit body.

Acting

The photographer positioned portable studio flash units on either side of the model. He used a No. 25 red filter to increase the glowing effect given by the infrared film.

Two light sources were used by a different photographer for a similar pose in this image. The diffused lighting aimed at the subject's left side was positioned high and aimed downwards. The pose, especially the half-hidden face, and the lighting gives the image an air of mystery.

Technical Details
6x6cm Medium Format Camera with a 150mm medium telephoto lens and Kodak TMax 100 b&w film.

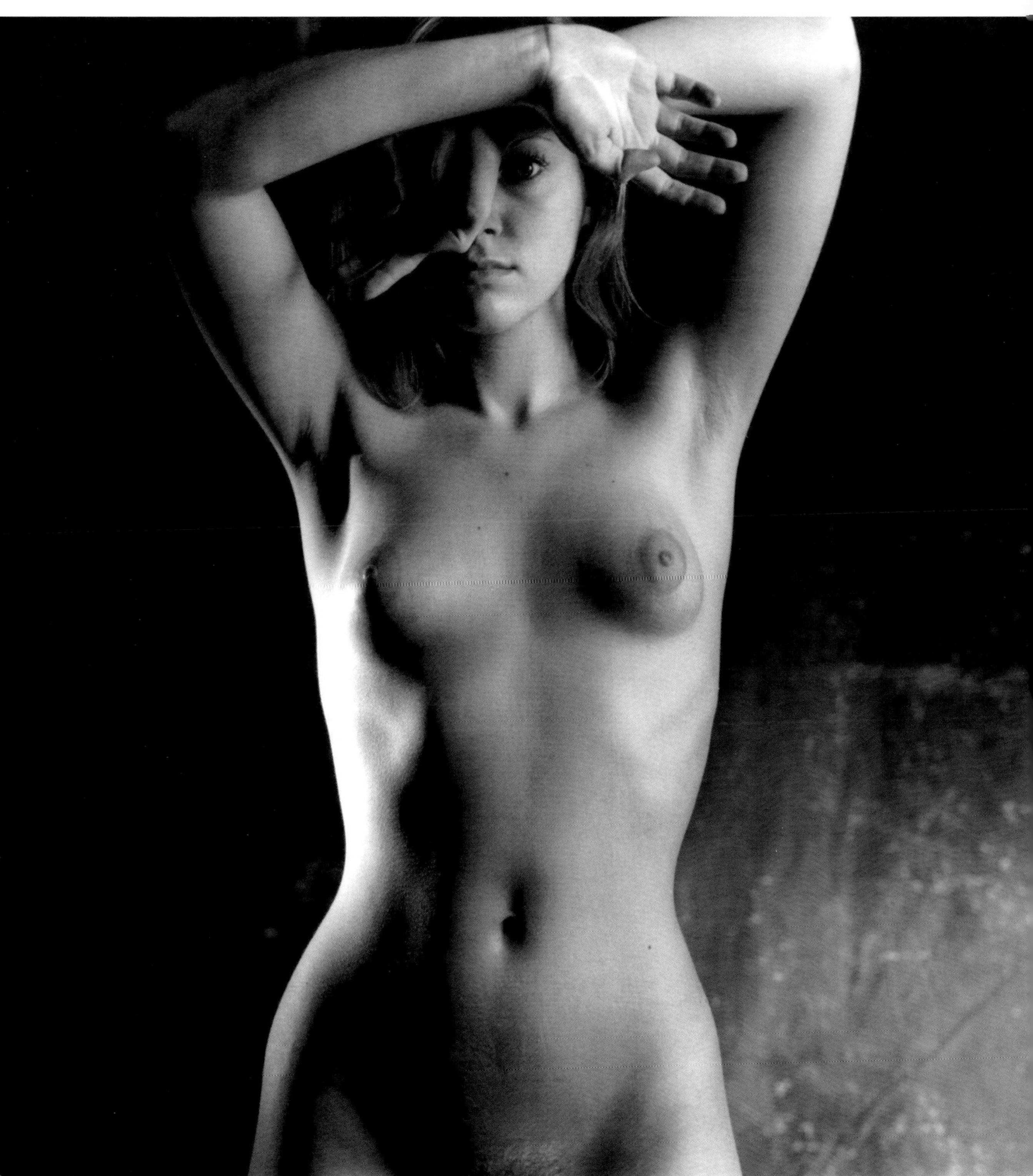

Photograph by Rene de Carufel

Full-length Nude

The human body stretched to its full length in a relaxed pose gives an impression of languor and luxury. The full-length nude can be treated compositionally in a variety of ways, either being used to fill the frame and create a sense of tension, or as an element in a more spacious composition where the feeling may be one of relaxation.

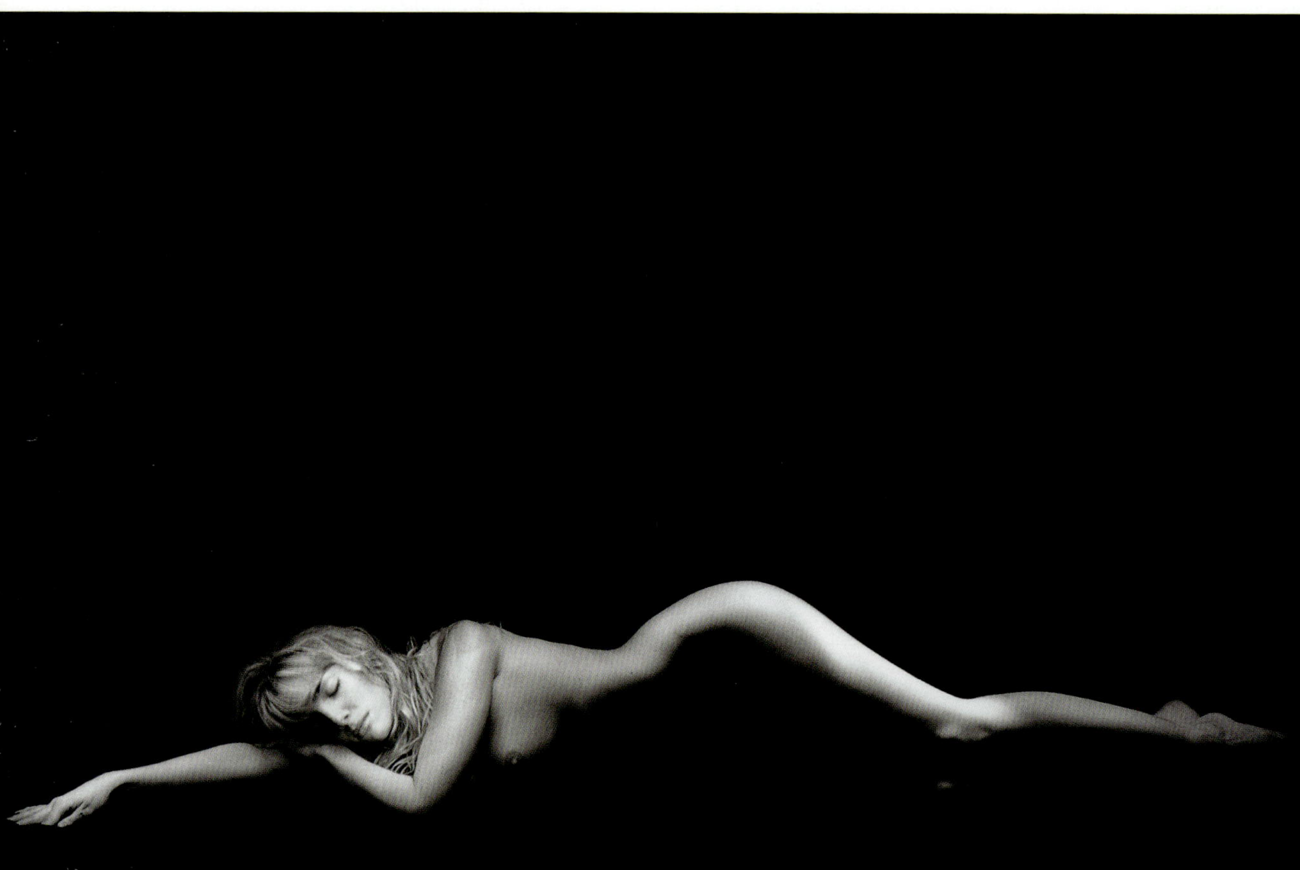

Technical Details
6x6cm Medium Format Camera with an 80mm standard lens and Agfapan APX 100 b&w film.

Photograph by Marc Jaffe

Seeing

Marc Jaffe used a light source with a narrow beam to 'paint' the subject with light while the camera's shutter remained open. He carefully pre-planned the image, working out how much illumination to give each part of the model's body.

Thinking

The idea was to create a high contrast effect to dramatically separate the girl's body from the dark background by outlining her outstretched form. Jaffe darkened the studio so that no other lighting intruded during the long exposure. This ensured that the background registered as a plain black area.

Acting

During the exposure time of one minute the photographer moved the light slowly across the model's body to provide even lighting. A little extra time was spent on illuminating her face and hair to bring out the detail in them.

Rule of Thumb

With the power that is available from today's studio lighting, trying to create an area of intense darkness can sometimes be a problem. Skilful use of power output and lighting accessories is one answer. But almost as important are dark, reflection-free surroundings. Black background paper or black velvet draped behind the model can help to intensify the shadows.

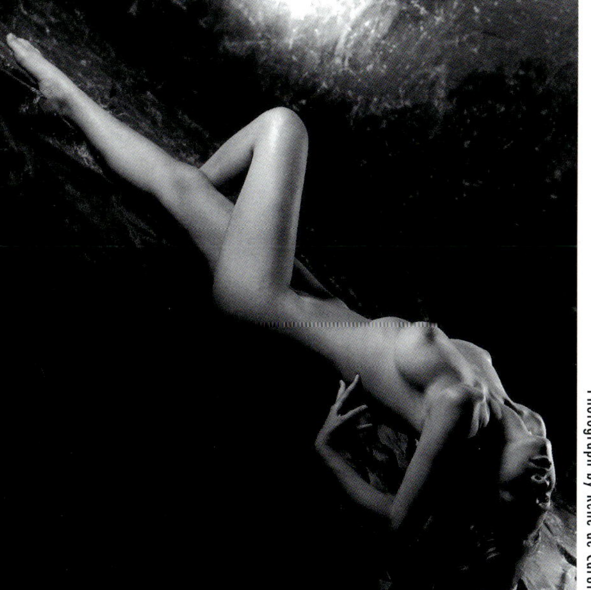

Photograph by Rene de Carufel

Rene de Carufel tilted the camera and framed so that the model's body, stretched out on the studio floor, filled the frame diagonally to create this dynamic composition. He added to the sense of drama by using bold lighting, with the model's face and much of the foreground in shadow while he picked out the background with a spotlight.

Technical Details

6x6cm Medium Format Camera with a 150mm telephoto lens. Fuji Velvia film was used for the original image, converted to a b&w print.

Action Shots

Models running, jumping or leaping in the air can make dynamic action pictures that evoke the athleticism portrayed in classical art. A fast shutter speed combined with flash can freeze movement and eliminate blur. However, the model need not actually be moving to create an impression of action: a careful pose and imaginative use of props can convey the idea just as well.

Photograph by Rene de Carufel

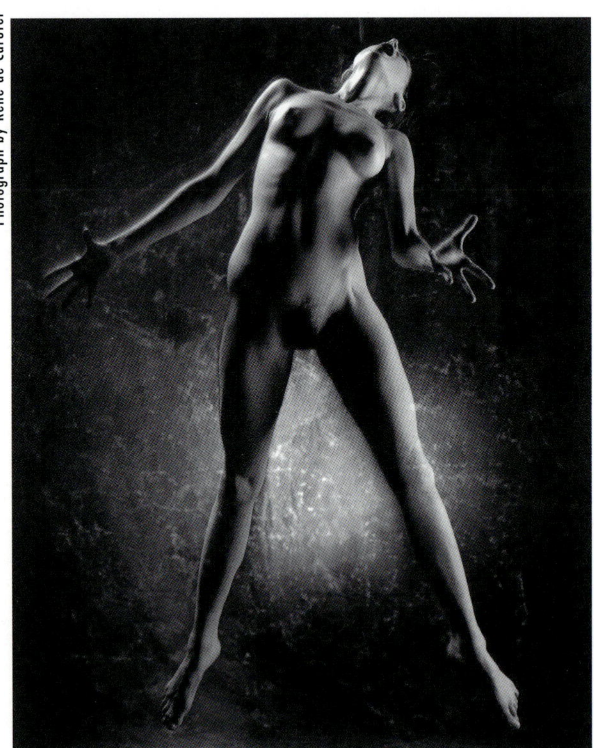

This was one of a series of shots the photographer tried of the model leaping into the air. The lighting set-up was similar to the one used for the picture on the right, but Rene de Carufel used electronic flash to freeze the motion. The tiny flash duration of a fraction of a second has recorded a moment where the model is effectively floating in mid-air.

Technical Details

6x6cm Medium Format Camera with an 80mm standard lens and Kodak TMax 100 b&w film.

Seeing

Rene de Carufel used a piece of rope as a simple yet effective prop, posing his model in such a way that she appears to be grappling with unseen forces outside the picture frame. He used the line formed by the rope and the model's arms as the basis of his composition, creating a strong yet fluid diagonal.

Thinking

The rope was secured outside the image area. The photographer framed the image so that the objects supporting the rope were hidden. He asked the model to tip her head back and shot the picture from a low viewpoint, suggesting a sense of tension.

Acting

A flash was placed high up to the right and slightly behind the model. A second flash was aimed at the background which suggests a marbled surface. The lighting trails off into darkness towards the edges of the frame.

Technical Details

6x6cm Medium Format Camera with a 150mm lens and Kodak TMax 100 b&w film.

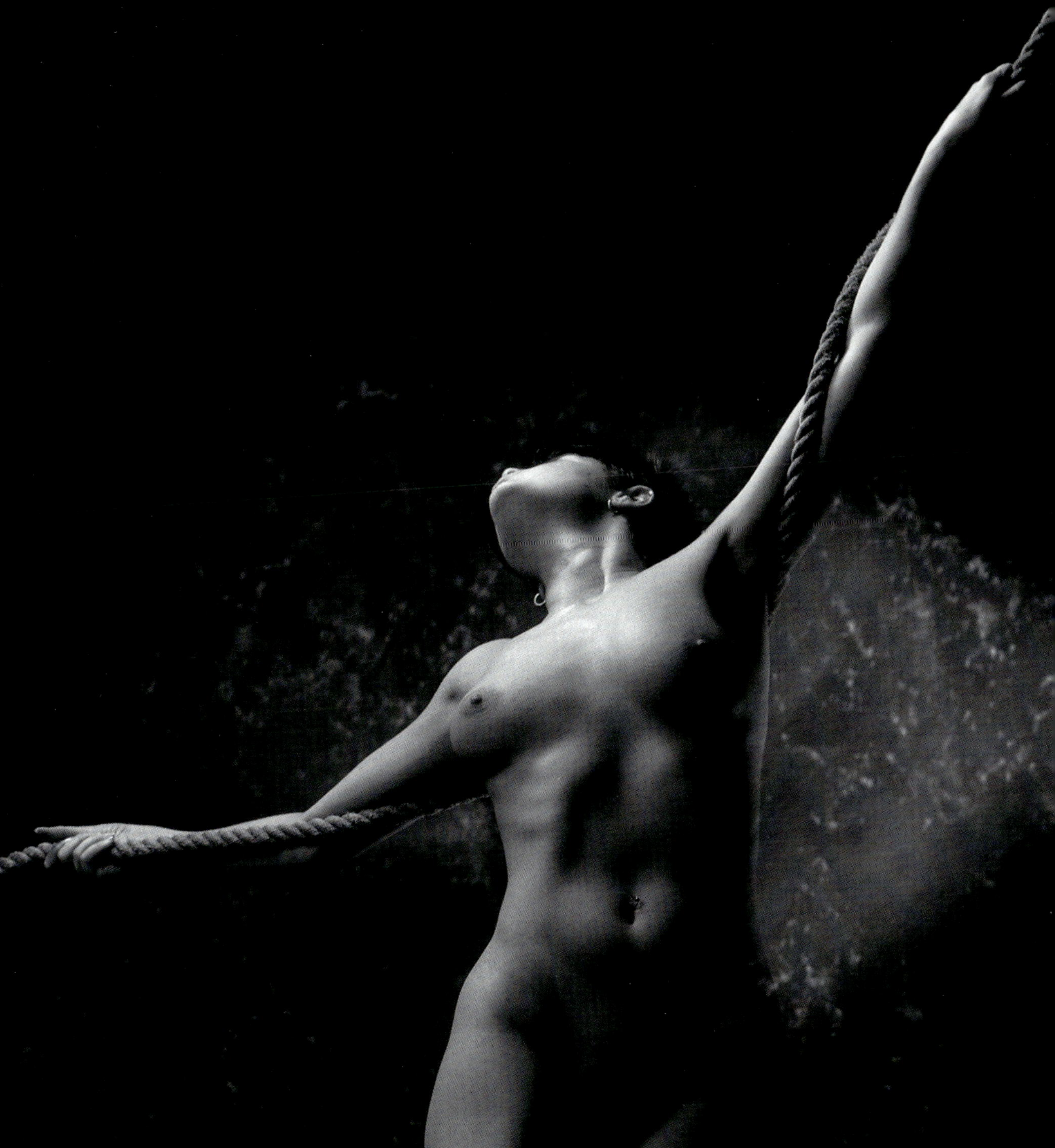

Photograph by Rene de Carufel

Mother-to-be

There are many types of nude, not all of which conform to conventional stereotypes of slender youth. Pregnancy creates a dramatic alteration of body shape which, when treated with sensitivity by the photographer, can produce an image with a beauty of its own.

Seeing

The photographer chose a plain studio background and a relatively simple lighting set-up to concentrate attention on the shapes and curves of the woman's heavily pregnant body. He created a 'halo' around her head by aiming a light at the background behind her. This gave the picture a semi-religious tone, intended to suggest the sanctity of motherhood.

Thinking

In contrast to the halo and the woman's serene expression, the photographer introduced a feeling of tension by having her adopt a squatting position. Her shaved head and African-style jewellery, together with the simple stone effect of the backdrop, were intended to suggest elemental forces. The combination of these different elements creates a very powerful image.

Acting

A spotlight created by a snoot placed over a studio light was aimed at the background to create the halo effect. Two lights were positioned an equal distance from the model, and were aimed so that they illuminated her but not the background.

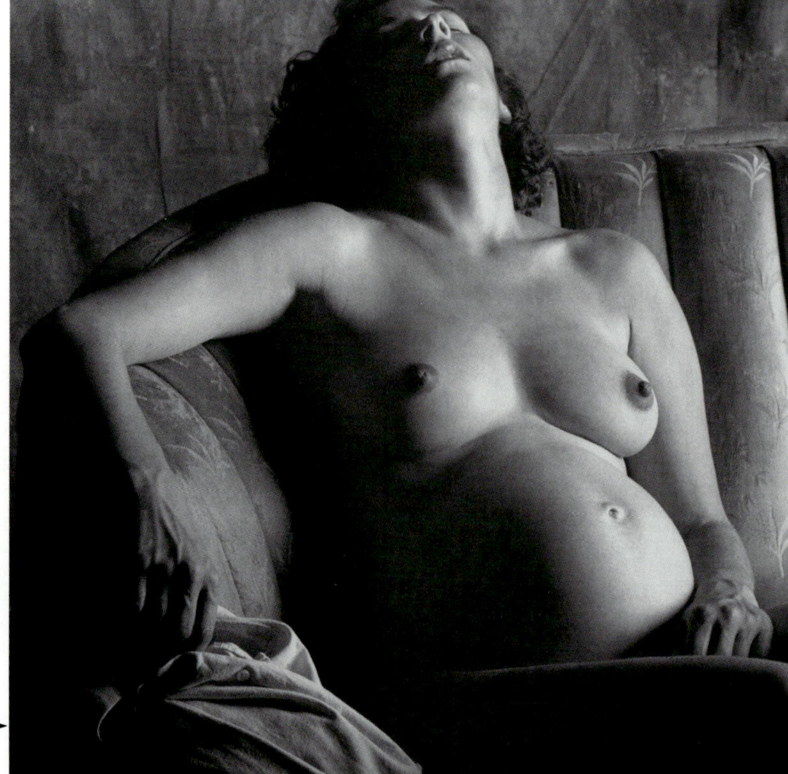

Photograph by Rene de Carufel

This study by Rene de Carufel gives the impression of being a candid taken by window light. It was actually taken in a studio with flash, carefully positioned to emphasise the subject's shape and form.

Technical Details

6x6cm Medium Format Camera with a 150mm lens and Kodak TMax 100 b&w film.

Technical Details
6x6cm Medium Format Camera with a 150mm lens and Kodak TMax b&w film.

Photograph by Rene de Carufel

Creating Visual Tension

A tilt of the camera, or a bold lighting effect, can create tension in a picture and give it a sense of drama. The effect can be created out of doors but is best suited to the studio, where the photographer has greater control over the composition and lighting of the shot.

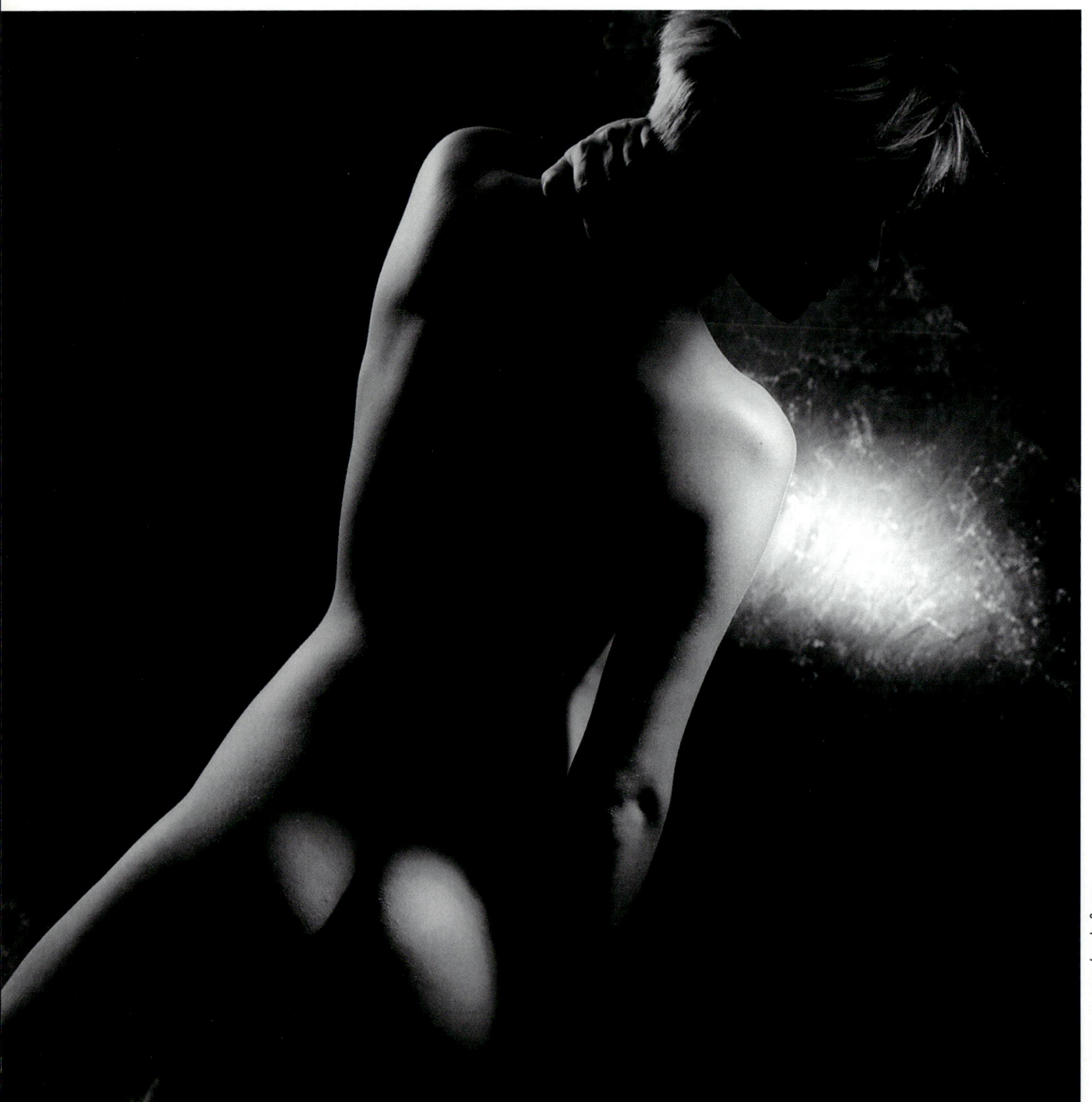

Photograph by Rene de Carufel

Seeing

Rene de Carufel was concerned here with exploiting the shape and form of the model's body rather than its details. He used her trunk to give a strong diagonal line to the picture, and stark studio lighting to create graphic contrasts between light and dark areas.

Thinking

The essence of this picture is the tension created by the disorientating tilt of the camera, which has a strong impact on the viewer's sense of perspective. The photographer used a fixed lighting set-up and then experimented with camera angles until he found the one he wanted. A tilt-and-swivel tripod head allowed him to lock the camera securely into position once he was satisfied and ready to take the picture.

Acting

A light set high and to the left of the model was positioned to outline her left side. A second light positioned high and to the right was aimed downwards towards her right shoulder. Finally, a third light was aimed at the background.

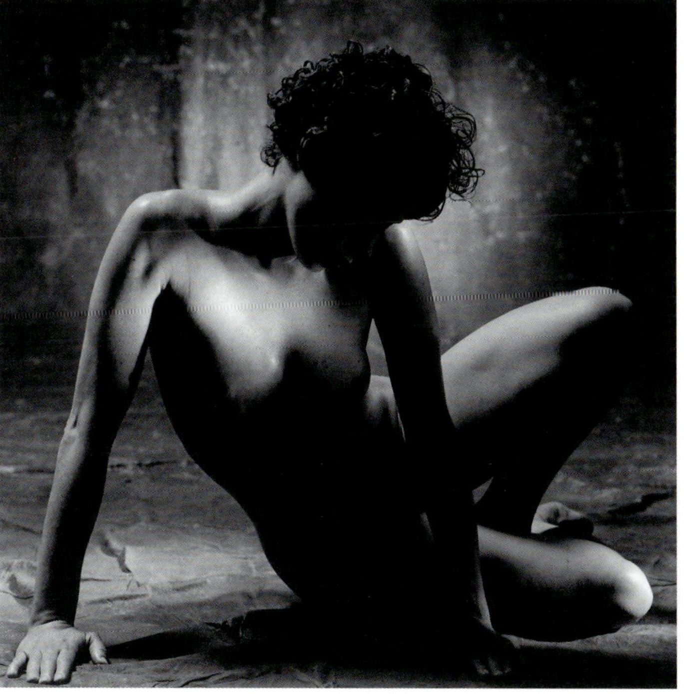

Photograph by Rene de Carufel

Narrow beam lighting, as used here, creates extremes of contrast. Here the photographer used it to pick out parts of the model's body, such as her legs and torso, while leaving her face hidden by shadow. Her meditative pose suggests that the picture has a story to tell, as if it was a scene from a narrative.

Technical Details

6x6cm Medium Format Camera with a 150mm lens and Kodak TMax 100 b&w film.

Technical Details

6x6cm Medium Format Camera with a 150mm lens and Kodak TMax 100 b&w film.

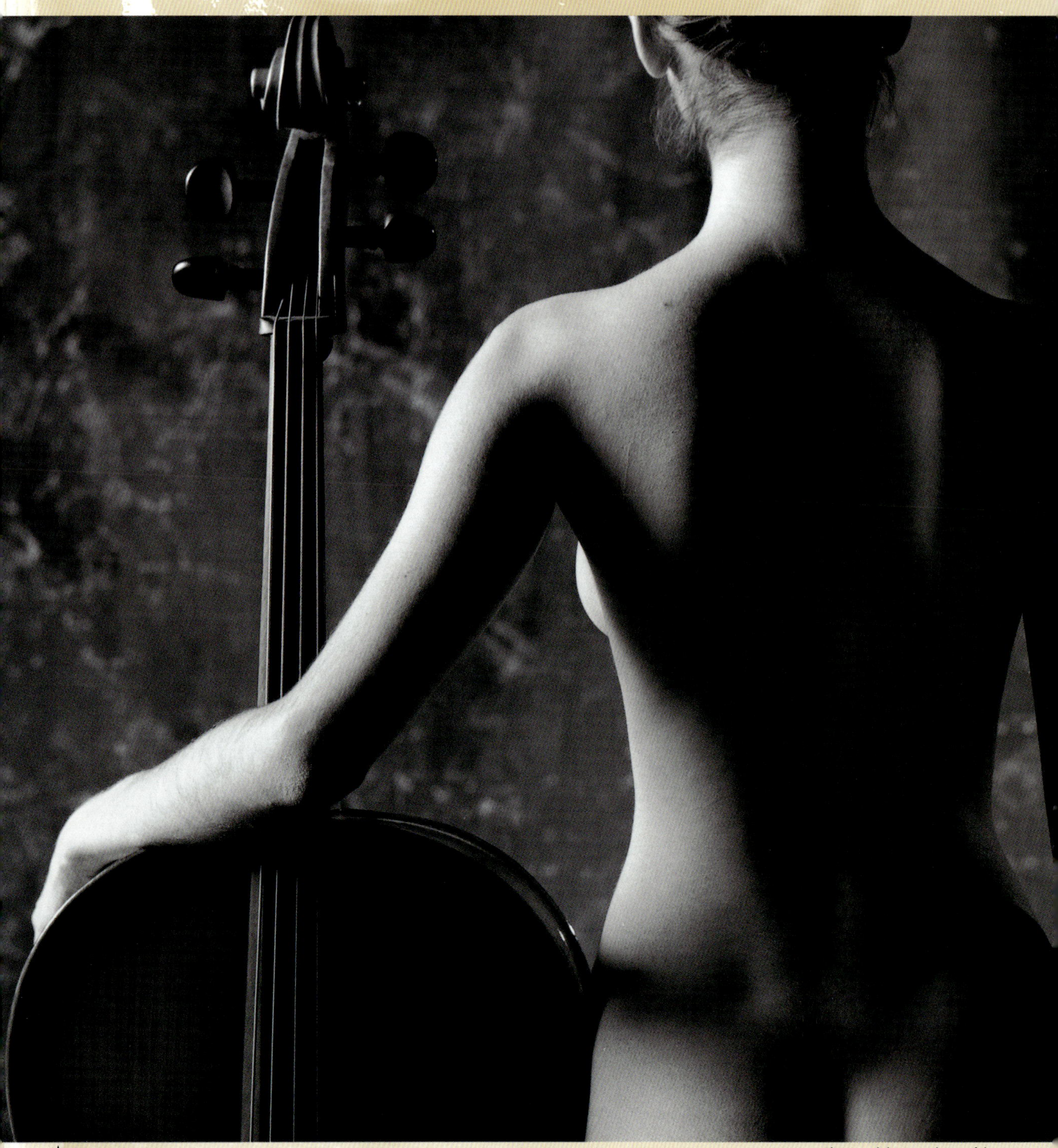

Technical Details
6x6cm Medium Format Camera with a 150mm telephoto lens and Kodak TMax 100 b&w film.

Photograph by Rene de Carufel

Seeing

This is one of a series of images Rene de Carufel took using a cello as a prop. The cello clearly echoes the model's torso, and the photographer placed them side by side to emphasise the similarity.

Thinking

Careful framing ensured that the girl's body and the cello were equally balanced. The photographer concentrated on the strong simple shapes at the centre of the image and framed accordingly, deliberately cropping out half the model's head.

Acting

A large softbox used as a sidelight picked out the hard and soft edges alike, creating highlights and areas of shadows. The neutral background was lit by over-spill illumination from the softbox.

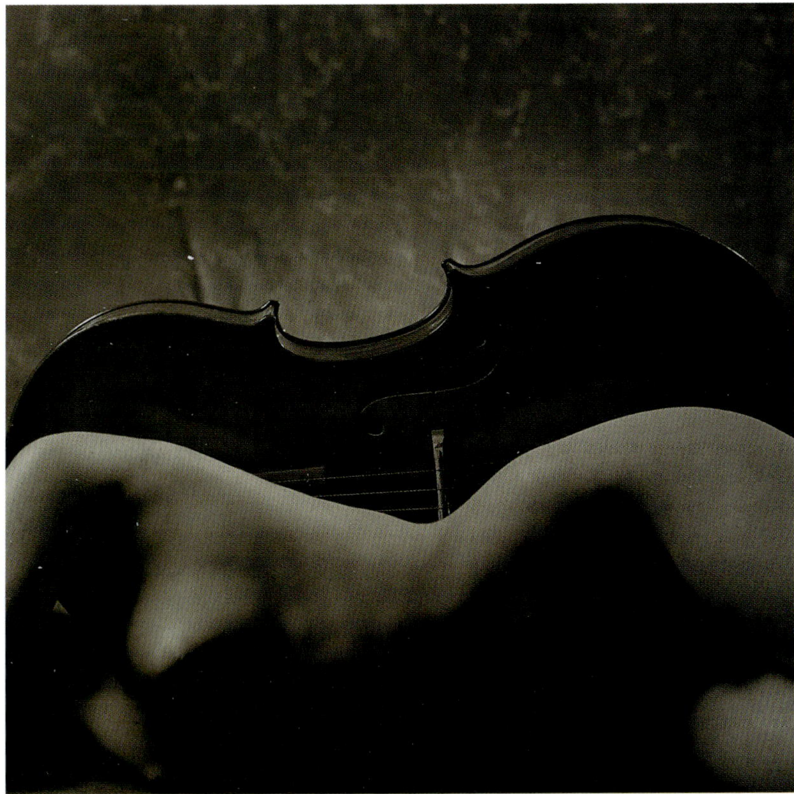

Photograph by Rene de Carufel

Rule of Thumb

A prop used with a portrait needs to be chosen with care. It has the potential either to enhance or detract from the photograph. A soft prop, such as material or fabric, can become one with the subject, being easily attached to the figure or draped over it. When a hard object is used as a prop, it's often most successful if it has a shape that will complement the finished composition.

In this semi-abstract image the photographer used a combination of low-key lighting and selective adjustment of tones at the darkroom stage to create a strong sense of mood.

Technical Details

6x6cm Medium Format Camera with a 150mm telephoto lens and Kodak TMax 100 b&w film.

Grace & Serenity

The human body at rest conveys a sense of grace, particularly if the body in question is that of a loose-limbed, athletic person caught in a moment of repose. Even though the person is sitting still, well-toned muscles suggest the presence of power and energy.

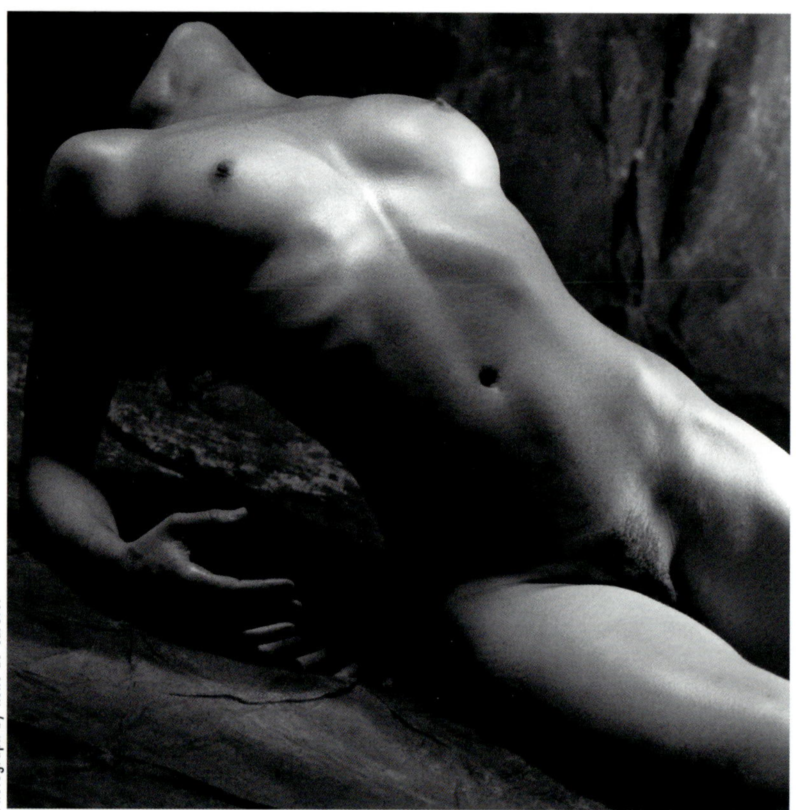

Photograph by Rene de Carufel

Another floor-based pose but one that conveys a totally different atmosphere. The lighting is dramatic and together with the model's pose, suggests a more physically active mood.

Technical Details

6x6cm Medium Format Camera with a 150mm lens and Kodak TMax 100 b&w film.

Seeing

This is one of a series of shots tried out by the photographer and model during a studio session. The model formed herself into a graceful, expressive shape.and one that suggests a dancer's pose.

Thinking

Lighting of this type is often used to light soft-textured objects and is ideal for conveying a mood of calm. The pale surroundings of the studio set reflected the illumination, maintaining a light and airy mood.

Acting

The photographer filled the frame with the girl. He placed a large softbox high and slightly to the front of the seated figure, adjusting it to give broad, even lighting which cast only soft shadows.

Rule of Thumb

Putting the model at ease is just as much a part of nude photography as the photographic skills involved. A relaxed model who is not feeling self-conscious will create poses that look more natural, and so increase the chances of a successful composition. Dancers, athletes and fashion models are often less self-conscious about their bodies than other models and, once the photographer has established a rapport with them, they make very good subjects.

Technical Details

6x6cm Medium Format Camera with a 150mm telephoto lens and Kodak TMax 100 b&w film.

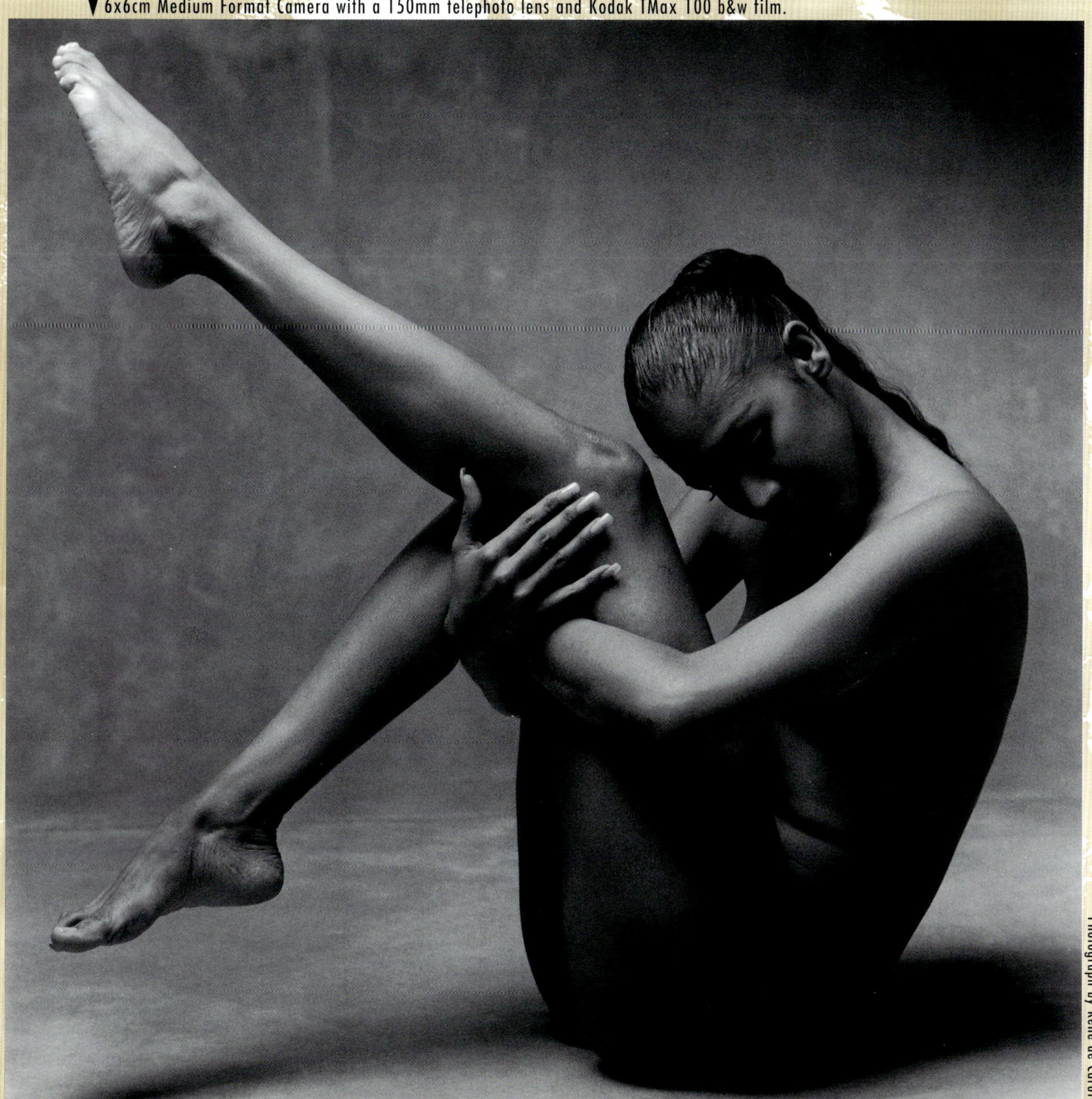

Photograph by Rene de Carufel

Darkroom Effects

The creation of a picture does not come to an end the moment the shutter button is pressed. Pictures can be manipulated even after the image has been recorded. For photographers working in black and white, the darkroom offers great possibilities for image enhancement, either in the way the picture is printed or in the way it is treated afterwards. Dyes, bleaches and colour toners offer a huge variety of possible effects.

Technical Details
6x6cm Medium Format Camera with a 110mm telephoto lens and Kodak TMax 400 b&w film.

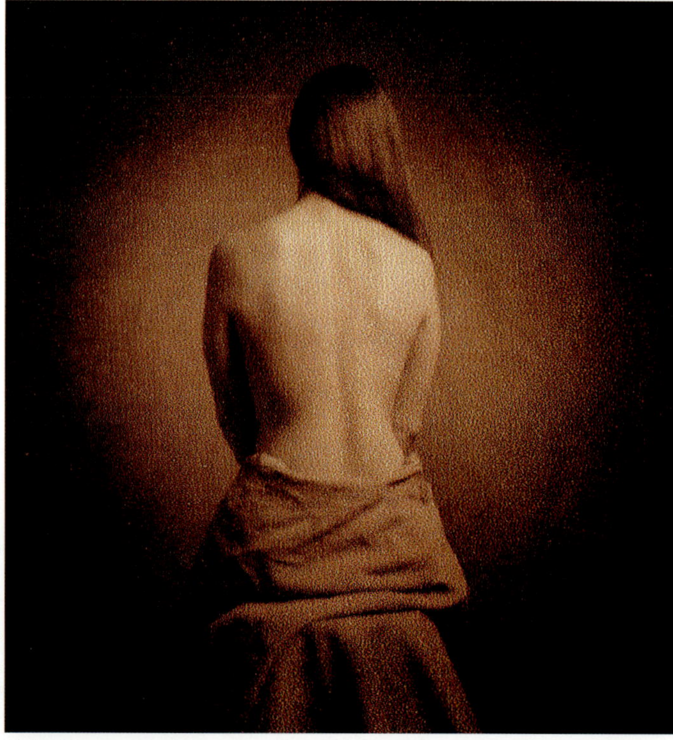

Photograph by Micheal Engman

Michael Engman used the same technique for this picture as for the one opposite but changed the model's pose to give a totally different feel to the image. The pose, the simple lighting and the coppery tint were all intended to create the impression of an antique photograph.

Seeing

Michael Engman wanted to give the impression that the girl was floating up through a liquid surface. He lit the picture with a single softbox placed directly above the model.

Thinking

As technically accomplished as the original image was, Engman wanted to make something more of it. So he manipulated the printing at the darkroom stage to create the effect he wanted.

Acting

Originally shot on black and white film, the negative was printed on to colour print paper through a plastic sheet which had a grain pattern on it. This procedure gave the final image a rich, coppery tone.

Rule of Thumb

Films with high ISO speeds tend to show more graininess than slower films. A grainy effect can also be produced by 'pushing' the film. This involves setting it at an ISO speed higher than its normal rating. The higher the ISO speed the stronger the grainy effect will be. Many photographers use this technique to add atmosphere to their pictures.

Technical Details
6x6cm Medium Format Camera with a 110mm telephoto lens and Kodak TMax 400 b&w film.

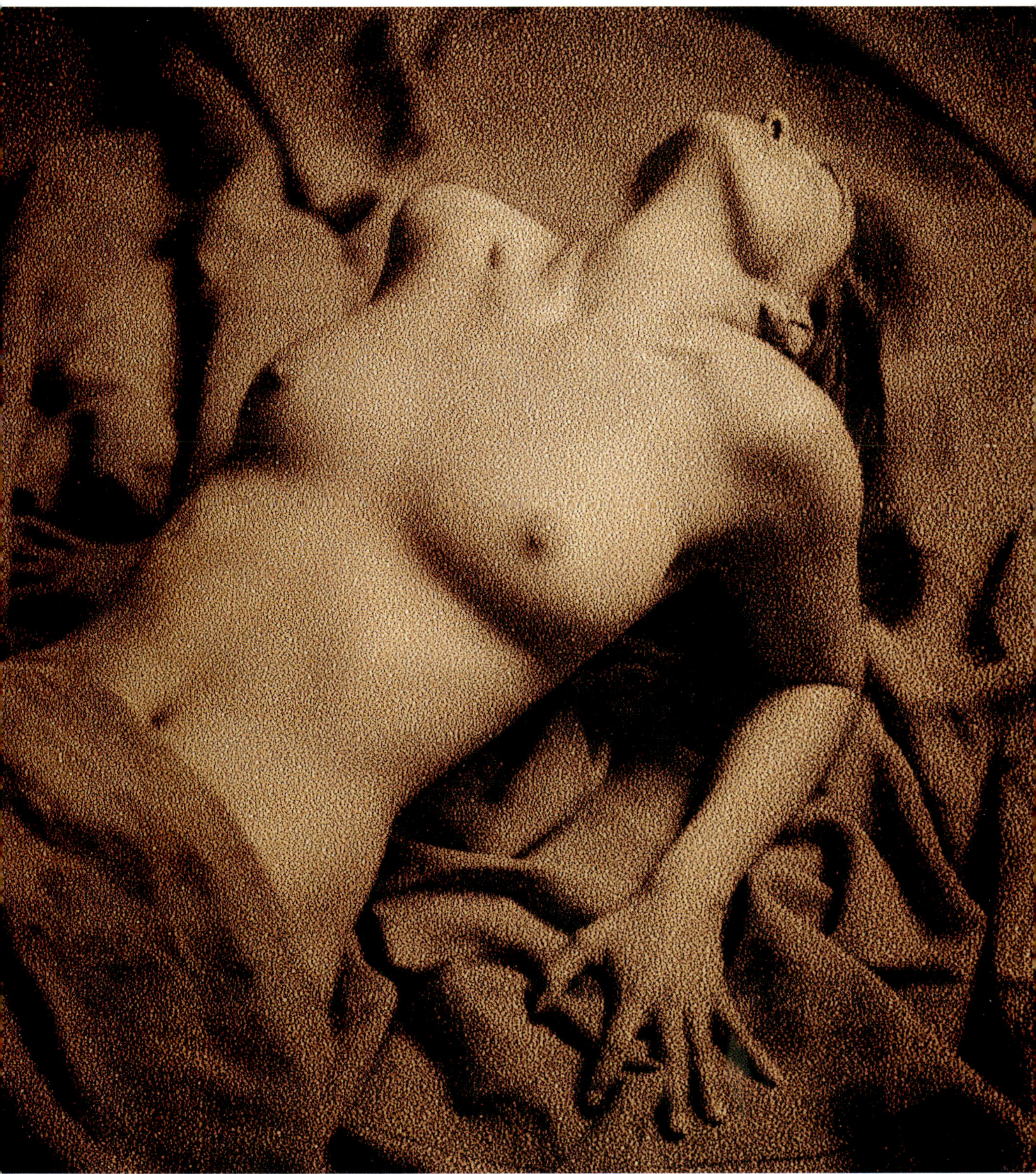

Photograph by Micheal Engman

Breaking the Rules

Rules are there to be broken. Always be ready to experiment with framing and lighting and imagine how each image could be made to look different. Don't be afraid to employ a little lateral thinking!

Technical Details

6x6cm Medium Format Camera with a 150mm telephoto lens and Kodak TMax 100 b&w film.

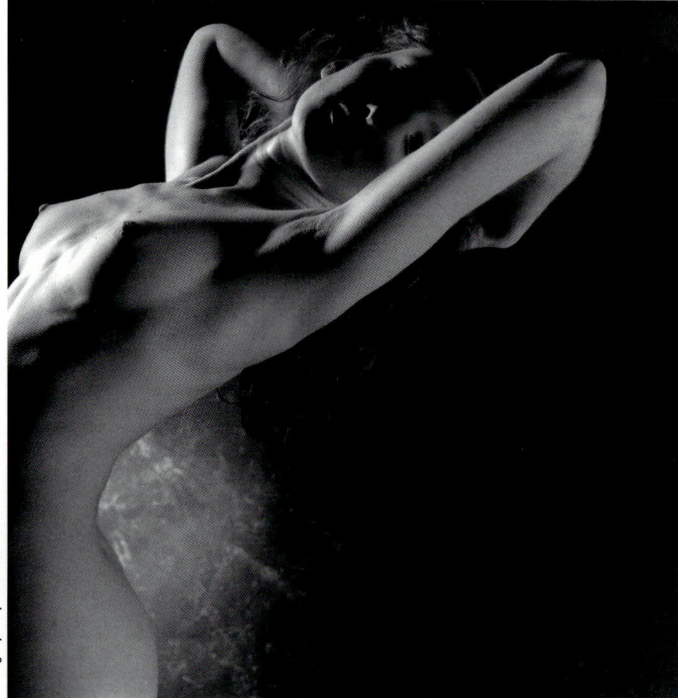

Photograph by Rene de Carufel

The model's pose and the large empty space to the right of her seem to break all the conventional rules of composition. Yet the shape formed by her arching body and the dark expanse beneath her combine to create impact. Three separate lights were used – one aimed towards the front of the model's body, one at her left side, and one at the background.

Seeing

Rules of composition provide a useful guide but here Rene de Carufel chose deliberately to disregard the conventions. Bending the rules need not lead to a reduction in impact. Sometimes it only increases it.

Thinking

The photographer created two distinct focal points within the same image – the model's face and the highlighted area of her back. This creates visual tension as the viewer's eye moves back and forth from one to the other.

Acting

A softbox positioned high up and to the model's right provided the main source of lighting. It also created a pinpoint reflection in the model's eye. This kind of reflection, known as a catchlight, provides a natural point of focus within the image.

Technical Details

6x6cm Medium Format Camera with a 150mm telephoto lens and Kodak TMax 100 b&w film.

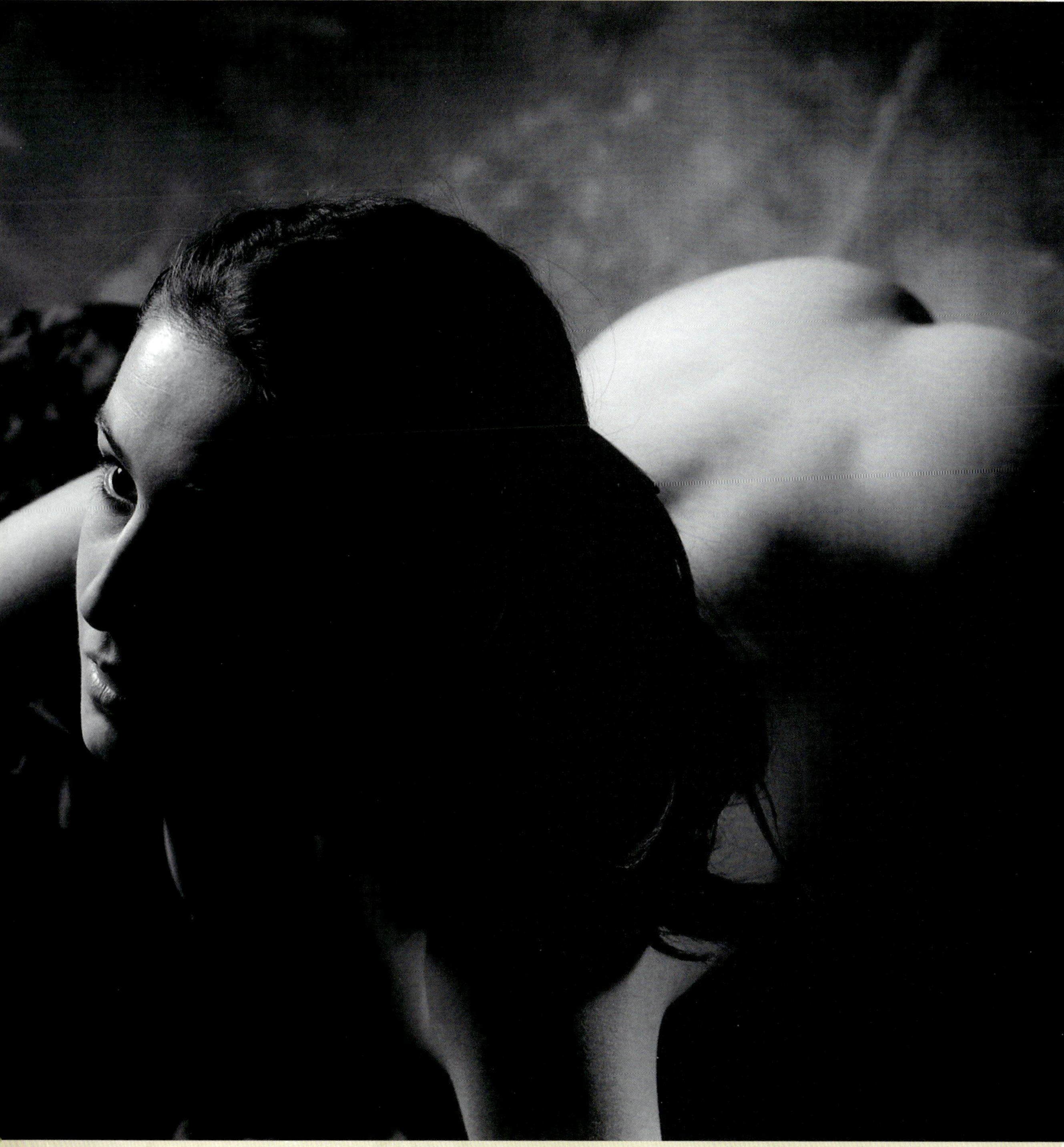

Photograph by Rene de Carufel

Selecting the Image

Every subject holds the potential for numerous different images. Shifting your camera position nearer to the subject or further away, using a wide-angle lens or a telephoto, selecting a wide aperture or a narrow one, or moving lighting from one position to another will all change the way the picture turns out. The changes may be subtle but each one in effect creates a fresh photograph.

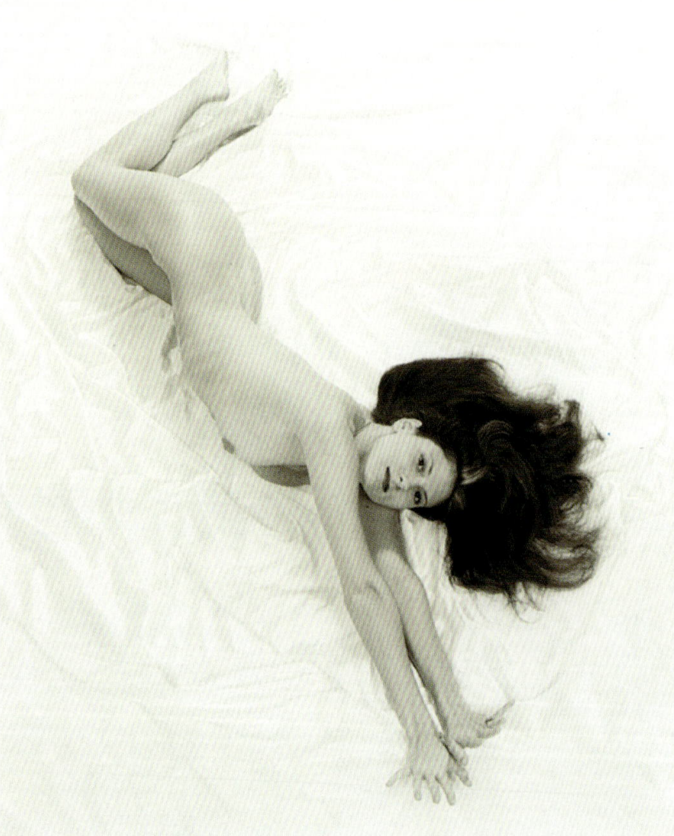

Seeing

A fixed lighting set-up together with tried and tested exposure settings allows for a relaxed photo session. Here it gave the photographer the time and space to experiment with framing and poses.

Thinking

A high-key lighting effect was created by using two large softboxes aimed downwards at the model. The light and airy effect was enhanced by the white backdrop reflecting light back at the model and filling in the shadow areas.

Acting

The girl's long hair was teased out to make it a more prominent element in the composition and to provide a contrast with the lightness of the rest of the image. The resulting black and white prints were then coloured with burgundy and gold toners to add warmth.

Technical Details

35mm SLR Camera with a 50mm lens and Kodak TMax 100 b&w film.

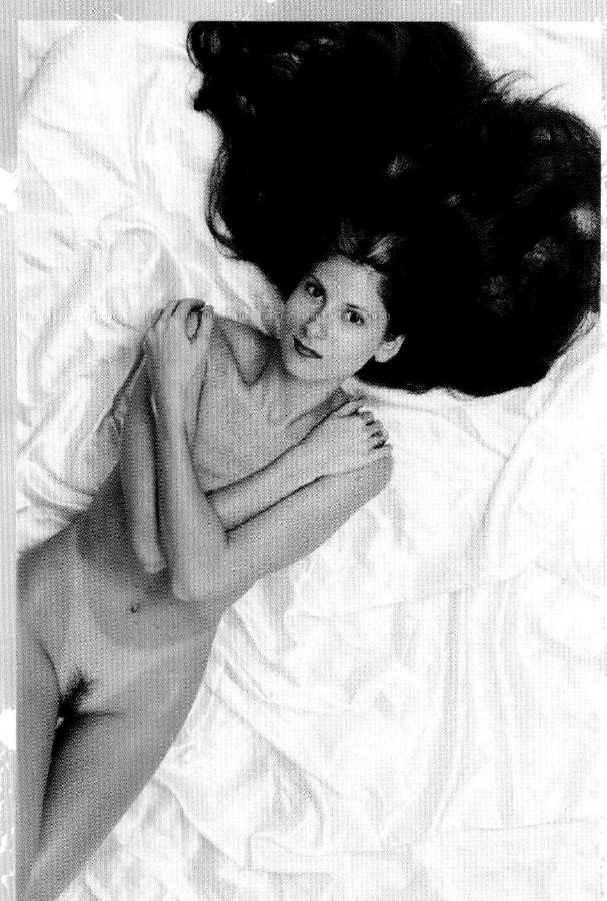

Apart from lighting, a factor that strongly affects the mood of a picture is the type of pose used. An adjustment of the limbs or a change in body position can create major or minor changes in the feel of an image. And simply changing to a different focal length of lens can give a different emphasis.

Technical Details

35mm SLR Camera with an 85mm lens and Kodak TMax 100 b&w film.

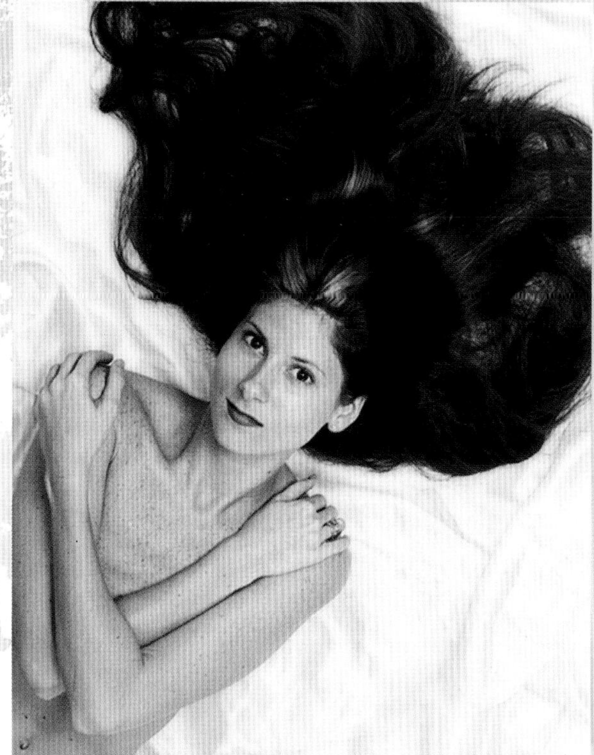

Despite the tilted angle, this is a symmetrical composition. The girl's face is at the centre of the photograph and her hair and body occupy roughly equal amounts of space. The telephoto lens used has flattened the perspective, reducing the perception of depth.

Technical Details

35mm SLR Camera with a 135mm lens and Kodak TMax 100 b&w film.

Toned Images

Toners are used to treat black and white prints in the darkroom and are available in a rich range of colours and densities. Careful choice of toner will enhance the overall look of the finished image.

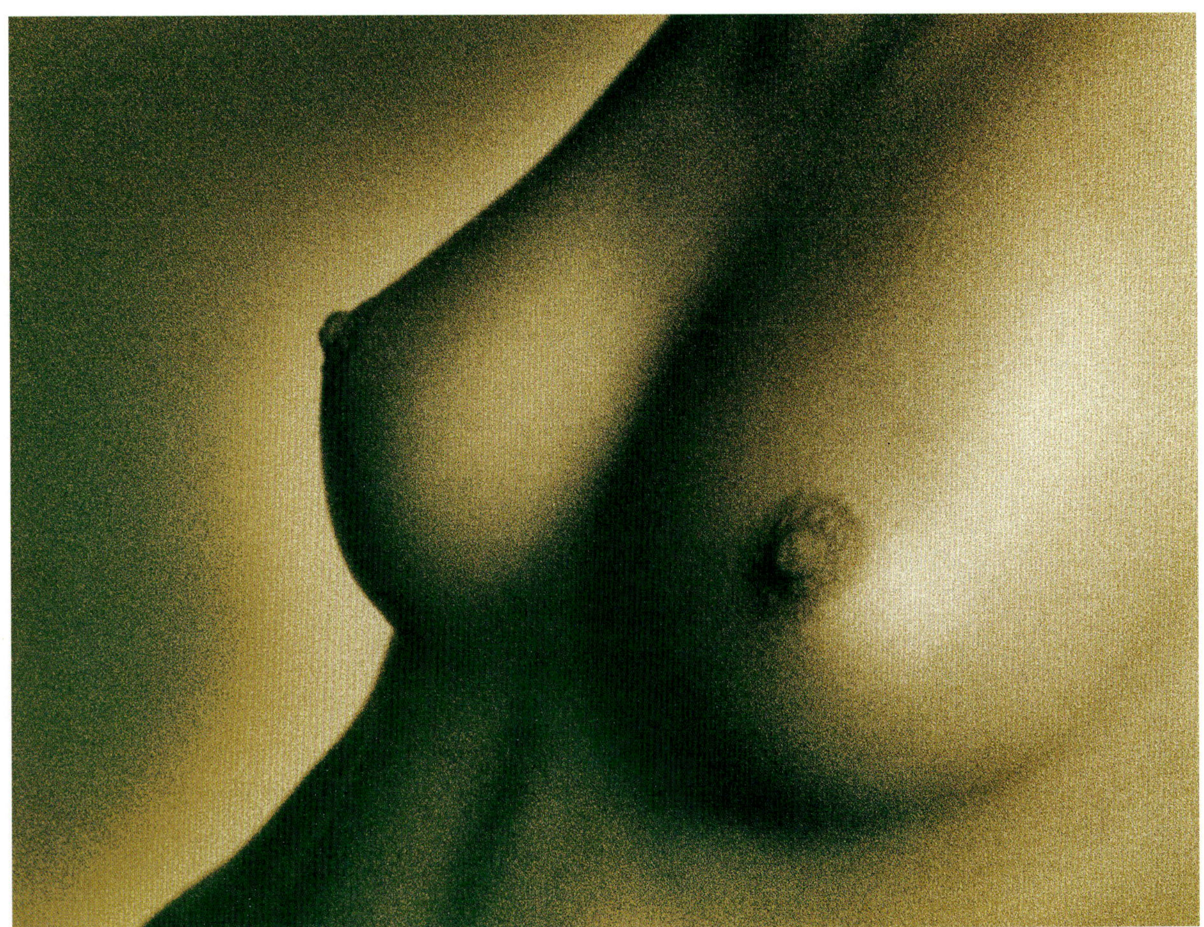

The photographer cropped in close to create a semi-abstract image but chose a different angle of view from the picture opposite. The sepia toning however is just as effective. As with the other print, the photographer used the technique of burning-in to darken the background area and define the outline of the subject more clearly. This is done while the paper is being exposed under the enlarger, before the print is developed and subsequently transferred to the toning solution bath.

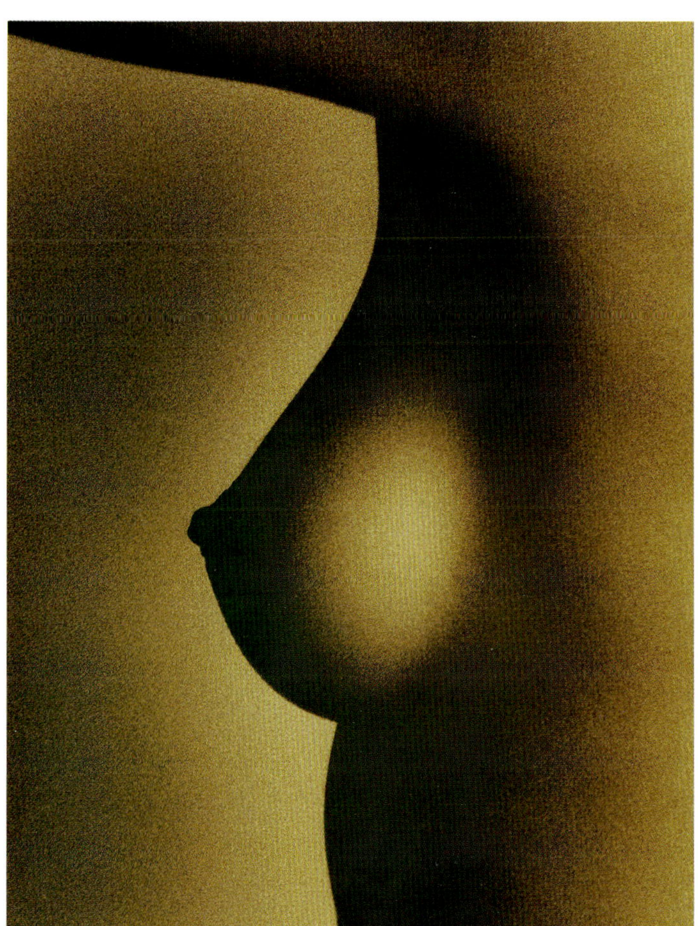

Technical Details

35mm SLR Camera with a 70–210mm lens and Kodak TMax 100 b&w film.

Technical Details

35mm SLR Camera with a 70–210mm lens and Kodak TMax 100 b&w film.

Seeing

The photographer used the curves of the model's arm and breast to create a simple yet graphic semi-abstract shot. This type of image often works best with toning effects as there are few extraneous details to distract attention from the overall look and feel of the image.

Thinking

Here the photographer set out with the finished image in mind and then shot the image to fit that pre-conceived plan. As toning affects the whole image the photographer needs to visualise the effect required and choose the colour of the toner carefully.

Acting

The soft shadowed lighting made the most of the rounded shapes. The real work was done in the darkroom, where the photographer used solutions to dye the image a warm sepia colour. He also used the technique of burning-in to darken the background area on the left. This involves masking off the main part of the image from the enlarger while the selected areas receive an extra period of exposure.

Rule of Thumb

Toning replaces black and white hues with the colour of the toning solution. A print with moderate contrast works best, as even its dark areas will be light enough to show the effect of the toner. Although toners come in a range of shades, it's the warm colours – and, especially the paler versions of them – that tend to be most effective with black and white prints.

Special Effects

Special effects can be created in-camera or by manipulation of the image after it has been taken. The simplest, yet some of the most effective, effects can be achieved through judicious use of props and lighting.

Seeing

Bryan Remer created a mood-filled study with the simple addition of a see-through scarf that had a black floral motif, but the material was flimsy enough to allow the body of the model to show through it.

Thinking

The fabric clung so closely to the model's body that it gave the impression of double exposure. The photographer emphasised the effect by keeping the background simple. He had the model lie on a plain piece of black felt spread out on the studio floor.

Acting

A softbox was positioned directly over the model's body, and this lit the subject without casting sharply defined shadows. The photographer used the telephoto end of a medium-length zoom lens to crop in tightly on the model's torso.

Technical Details

35mm SLR Camera with a 35–105mm zoom lens and Kodak TMax 400 b&w white film.

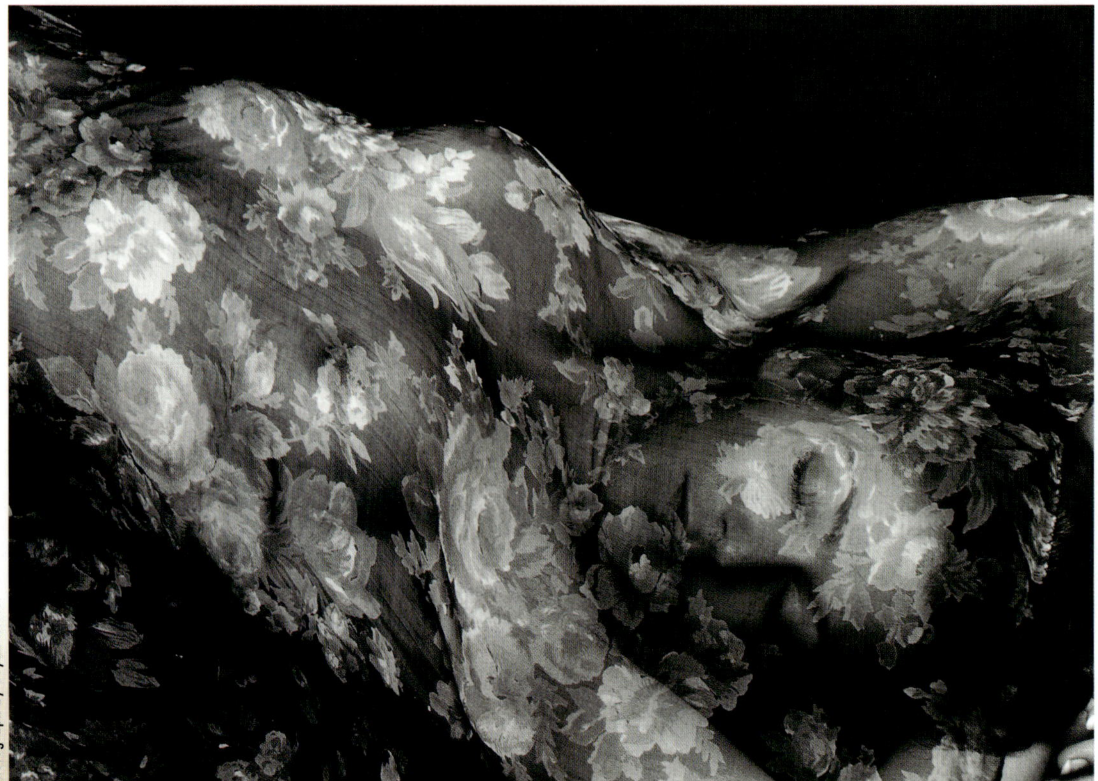

Photograph by Bryan Remer

Technical Details

▼ 35mm SLR Camera with a 50mm standard lens and Kodak b&w Recording Film.

A black background and a large softbox were the simple ingredients for this shot. The grainy effect is a characteristic of the film that was used, Kodak Recording Film.

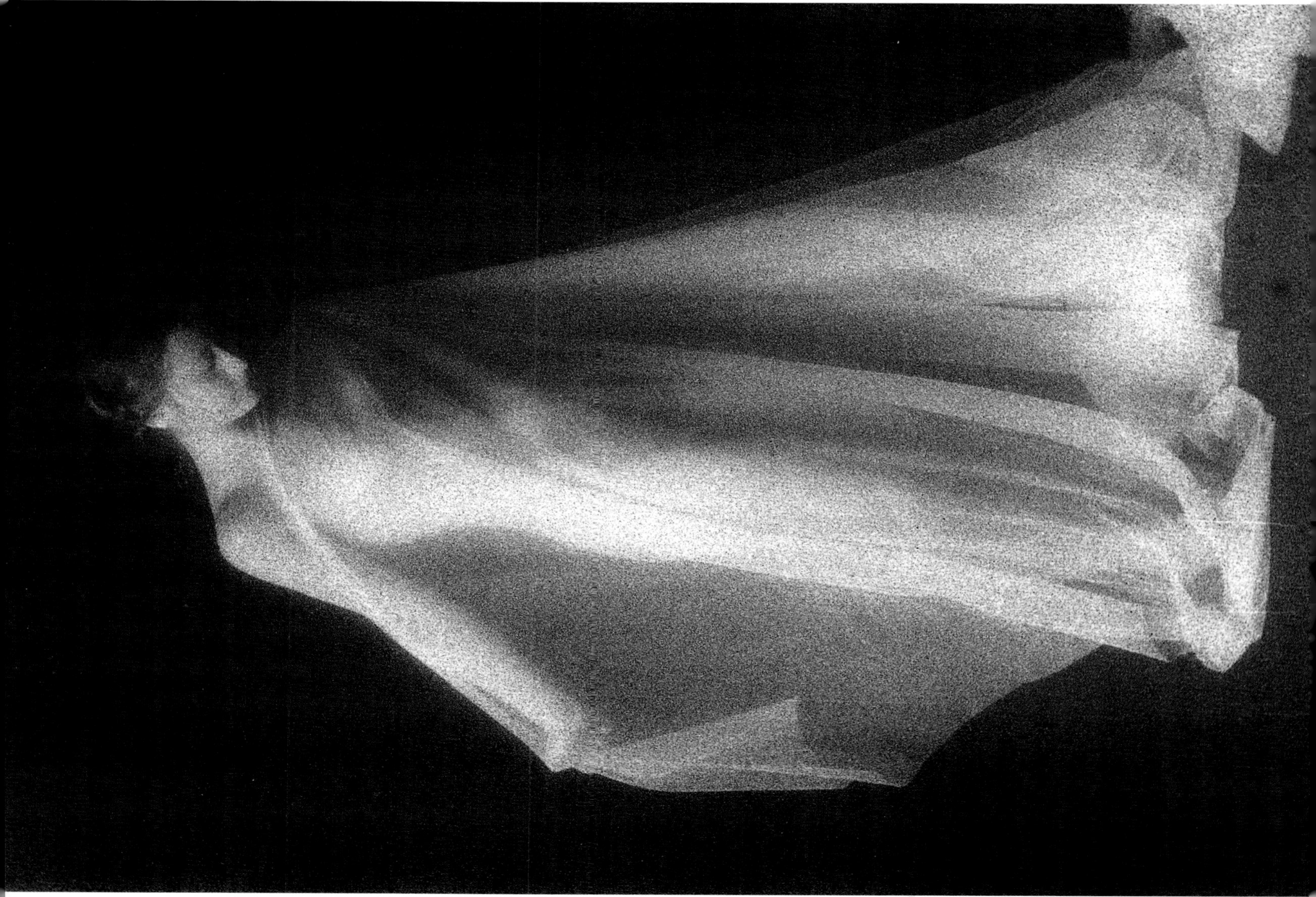

Soft & Hard Light

The same subject can be portrayed very differently by varying the quality of the lighting used to illuminate it. Soft lighting produces even tones and a mood of gentleness while harder lighting accentuates angles and creates a more dramatic image.

Seeing

The photographer wanted an image in which the contours of the female form created a semi-abstract image through use of selective lighting. He chose soft, even illumination and made it directional, creating contrast which emphasised the shape and form of the model's body. Overall, he was aiming for an effect that suggested the experimental photography of the 1930s.

Thinking

He used the background as a compositional element by directing a broad diagonal band of light across it, positioning a light low down to the model's right and angling it upwards. This adds a sense of depth to the picture and complements the highlighted areas on the model's shoulders, buttocks and arms.

Acting

Using a 35–70mm zoom lens, the photographer experimented with different ways of framing the image, eventually settling on this bold crop. By excluding her head and legs, he focused attention on the shape of her body. He exposed for the highlight areas, picked out by a flash unit placed to the model's right, meaning that certain areas were cast into shadow.

Technical Details

35mm SLR Camera with a 35–70mm zoom lens and Fujichrome 100 colour transparency film.

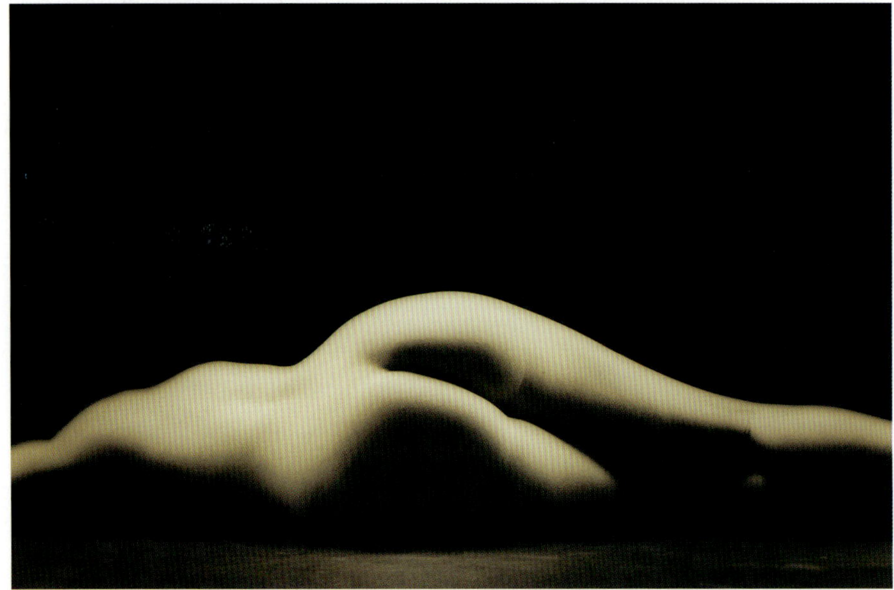

The lighting and the pose have reduced the nude torso to a series of curved and rounded shapes. The strong lighting and high contrast make the shapes stand out from the black background.

Technical Details

35mm SLR Camera with a 35–70mm zoom lens and Kodak TMax 400 b&w film.

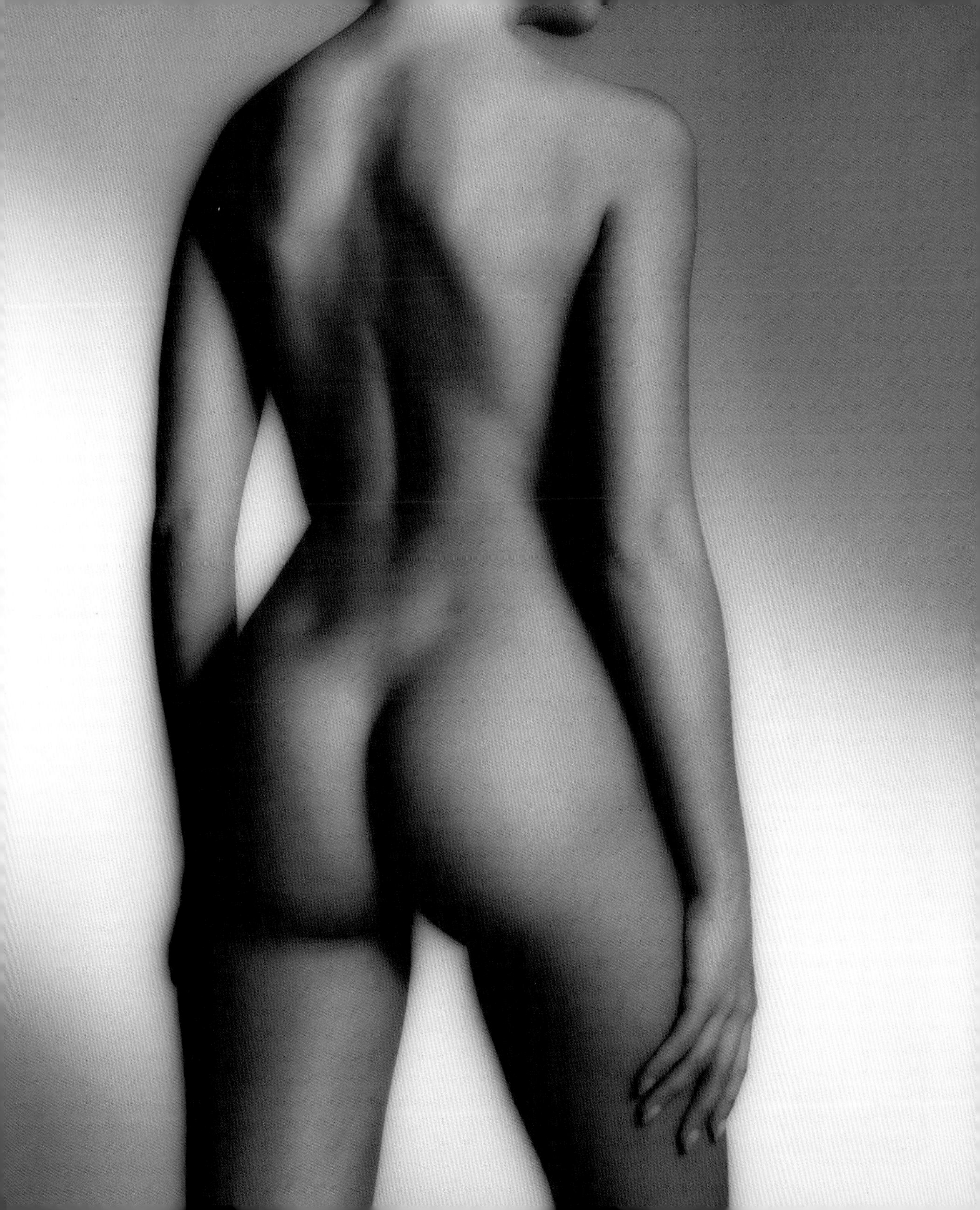

Colouring the Image

Images can be given a rich range of tones and colours by treating them in toning solutions in the darkroom. Alternatively, colour can be introduced at the initial picture-taking stage by using body paint applied directly to the model's skin.

Technical Details

35mm SLR Camera with a 210mm telephoto lens and Ilford Plus-X b&w film.

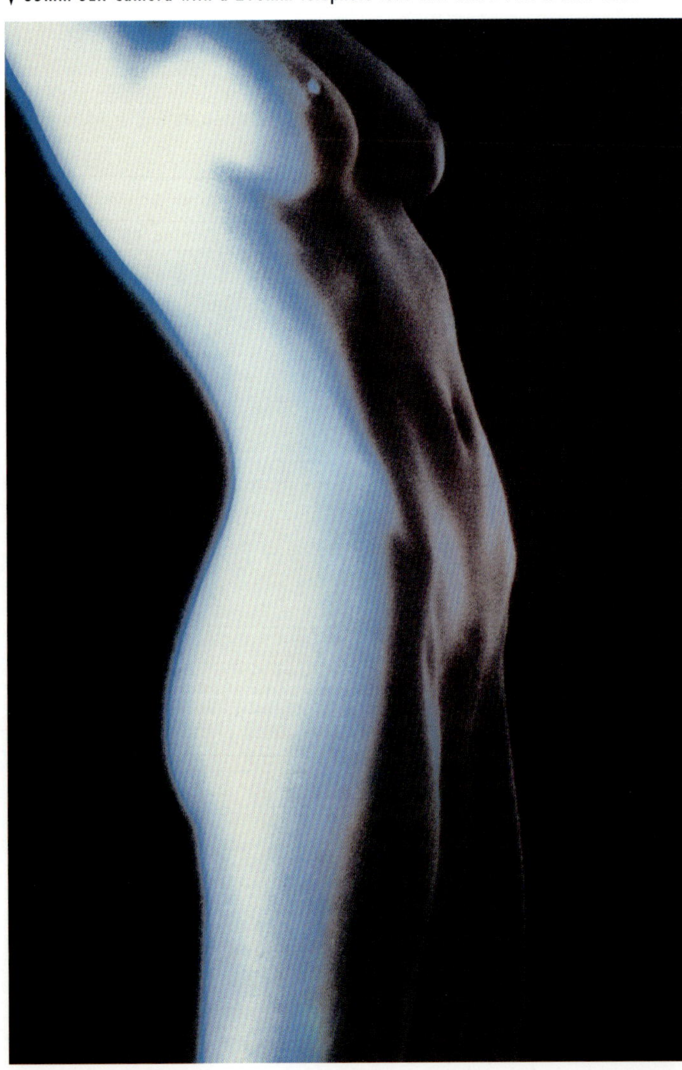

Seeing

Photographer Bob Norris created this image as part of a personal project. His intention was to produce the likeness of a golden idol.

Thinking

The photographer covered the model from head-to-toe in special make-up which helped create the impression of a gilded statue. The background material was chosen especially to create an exotic atmosphere.

Acting

The set-up was photographed using black and white instant film. The high ISO speed of this type of film means that it gives a noticeably grainy negative. The resulting black and white print was then toned in the darkroom.

The original of this image was a black and white print which was put through blue toning solution. The photographer created the solarised effect by exposing the printing paper to a short burst of light in the darkroom, after the image had been exposed but before it had been developed or run through the toning bath.

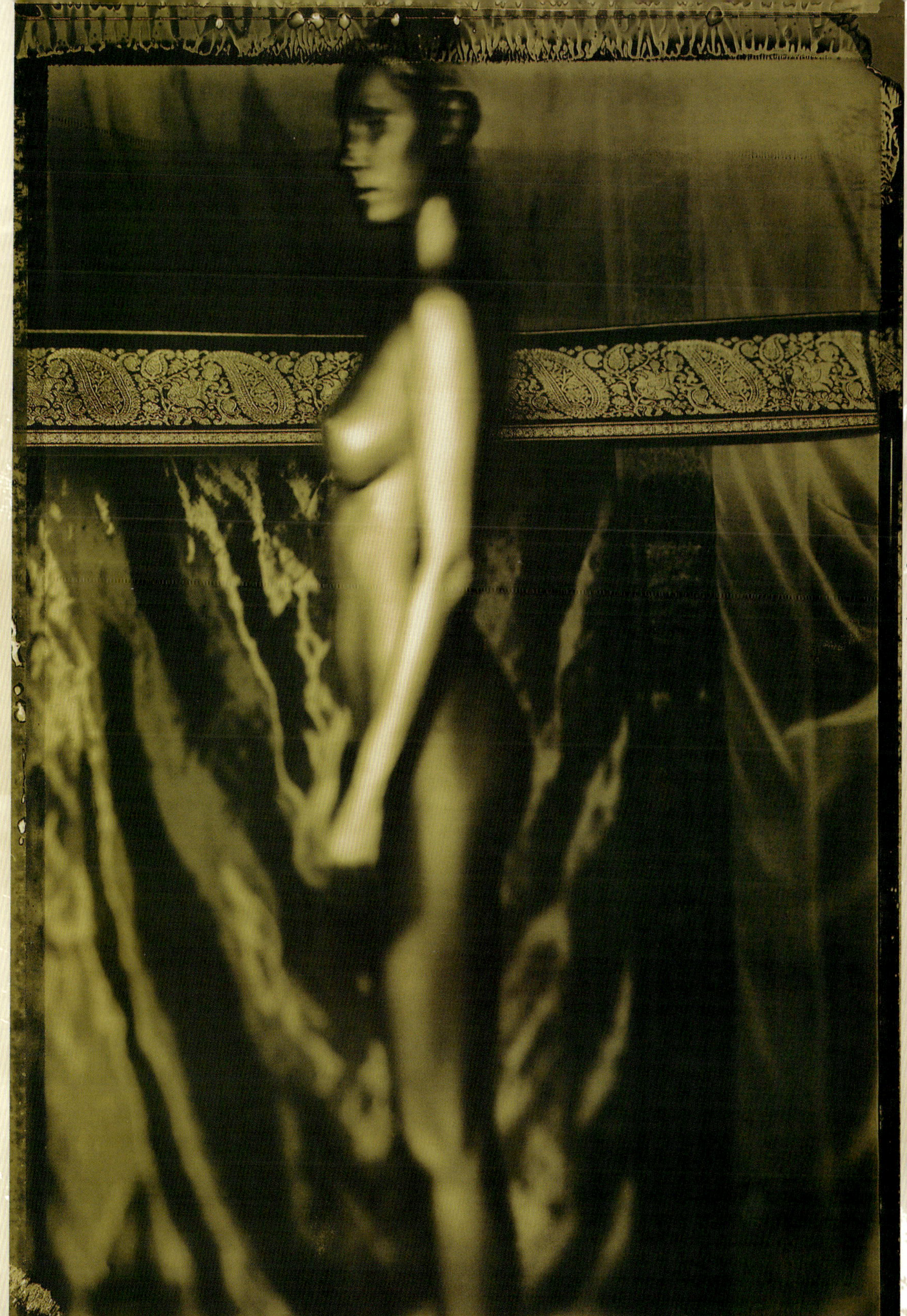

Technical Details

35mm SLR Camera with a 105mm telephoto lens and b&w film with a high ISO speed.

Photograph by Bob Norris

Fabric as a Prop

Fabrics such as silk and velvet can be deployed as backgrounds or draped around the model's body to give a sense of luxury and sensuality. Used effectively, they can evoke the poses of classical statuary or the feel of Old Master paintings.

Technical Details

35mm SLR Camera with a 105mm telephoto lens and Ilford Plus-X b&w film.

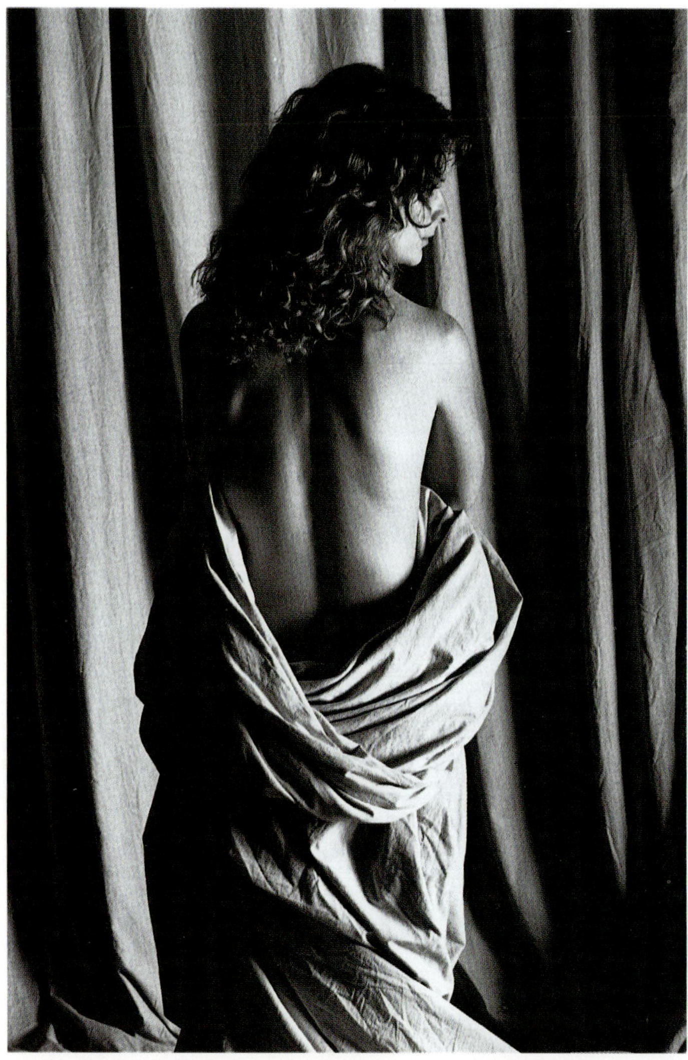

Seeing

Inspiration can come from the simplest of elements. Here the photographer used some of the background material as a drape around the model's torso.

Thinking

The fabric acts as a link between the model and the background. The photographer intended the folds of the material and the model's pose to provide an echo of classical paintings and sculpture.

Acting

A large source of light was aimed at the model's right side, and a reflector placed at the left was used to fill in some of the shadow areas. A short telephoto lens was used to fill the frame and flatten the perspective, making model and background appear close together.

Rule of Thumb

Fabric is a popular choice as a prop for nude portraits. The choice of material will play a significant part in the finished image. A thick, heavy cloth such as velvet can be draped around the figure. A thinner cloth such as silk or muslin enables parts of the figure to show through. Such a fabric may also have a printed design that complements the nude or the setting.

For the image on the right, Michèle Francken painted the background glossy silver so that it acted like a giant reflector. One main light was aimed at the model's left-hand side. Its positioning and intensity were intended to give the effect of sunlight. The 'tattoo' on her back was created by painting on a design with henna.

Technical Details

▼Medium Format Camera with Polaroid positive/negative b&w film.

Photograph by Michèle Francken

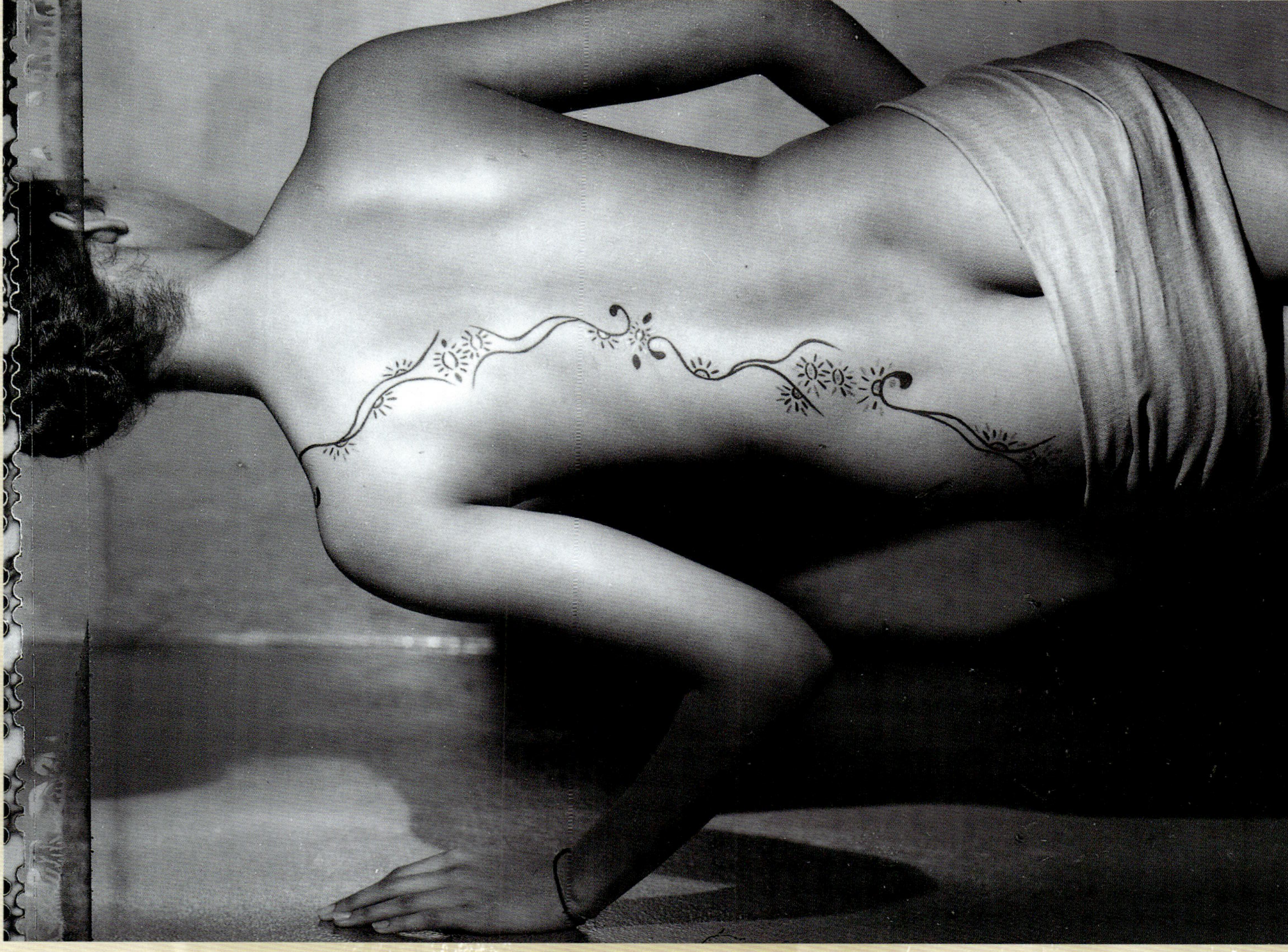

One Model, Two Moods

A model can seem to be a completely different person from one image to the next if the pose, lighting and composition are varied. The skilled photographer is able to visualise precisely the desired image and then use the model and set as a blank canvas on to which this vision is projected.

Technical Details

35mm SLR Camera with a 35–70mm zoom lens and Kodak TMax 400 b&w film.

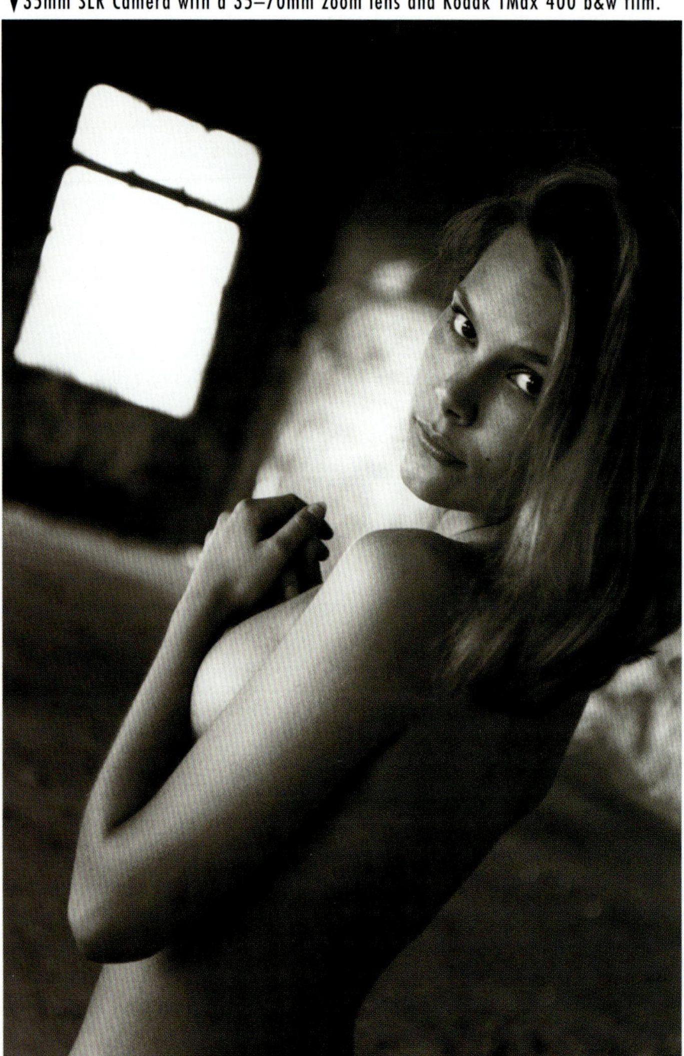

Seeing

There is a certain amount of tension in this shot, created by the bold framing which creates a virtually diagonal composition. At the same time, the model's challenging glance at the camera communicates directly with the viewer.

Thinking

Bright overcast daylight gives fewer extremes of contrast than light coming from a bright and cloudless sky. So, though there are strong shadows in this image, the detail is good even in the dark areas. The simple piece of fabric draped over the model acts as a prop, simultaneously concealing and revealing her body.

Acting

The photographer took a straightforward exposure reading from the girl's face, using his 35mm camera's built-in metering system. He used a short zoom to crop in tight and crouched down to shoot from a low angle, magnifying the sense of drama in the shot.

The sources of illumination – windows both in and out of shot – are far away and soften the highlight and shadow areas. The model's expression is soft and relaxed too, without the tension she shows in the shot on the right.

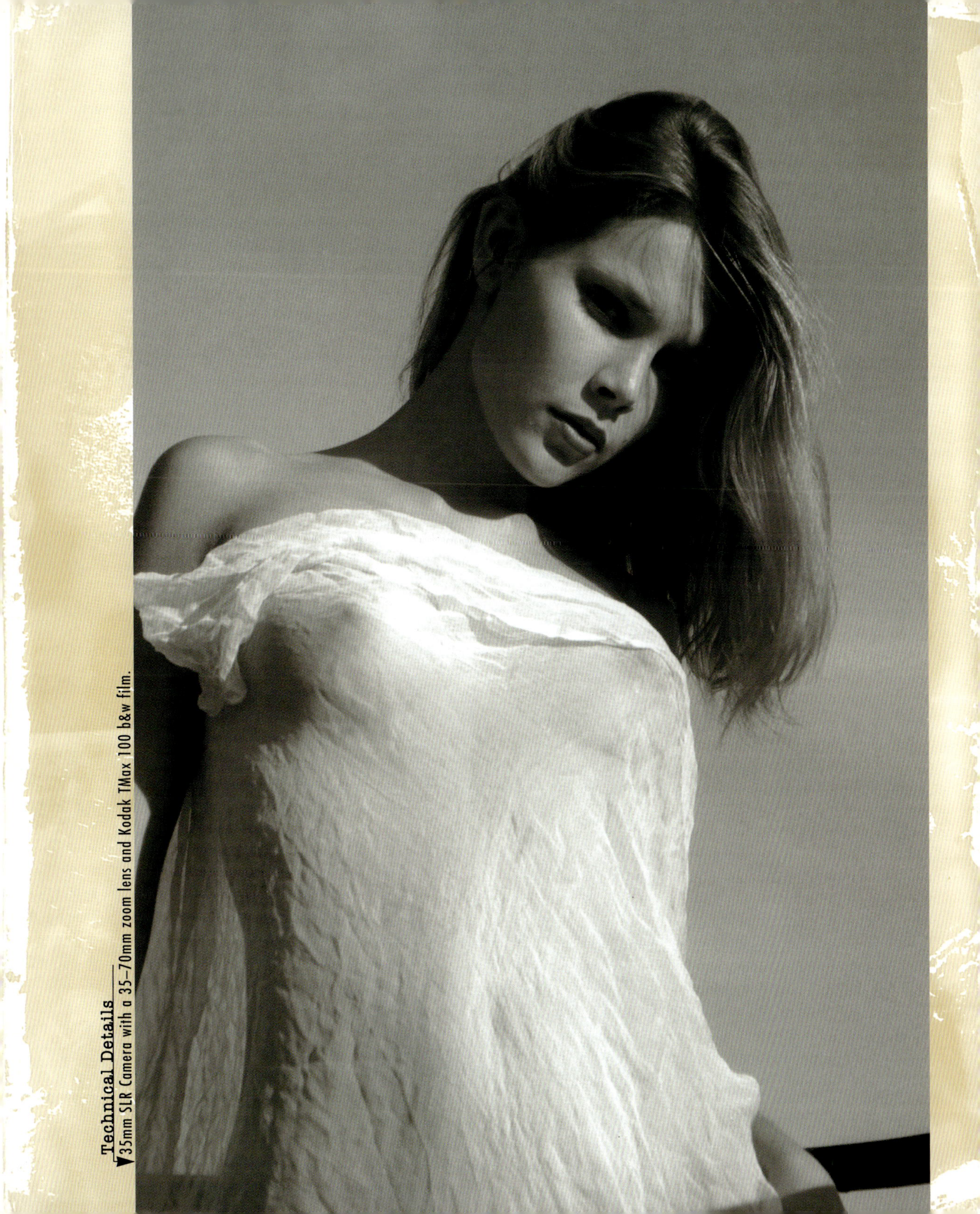

Technical Details
35mm SLR Camera with a 35–70mm zoom lens and Kodak TMax 100 b&w film.

Light & Dark

The contrast between light and dark is a strong compositional device. A studio set-up can be used to create solid areas of darkness within the image, which act as a frame for a model whose body is highlighted by selective lighting.

Technical Details

35mm SLR Camera with a 28–70mm zoom lens at a 35mm setting and Ilford XP-2 chromogenic b&w film.

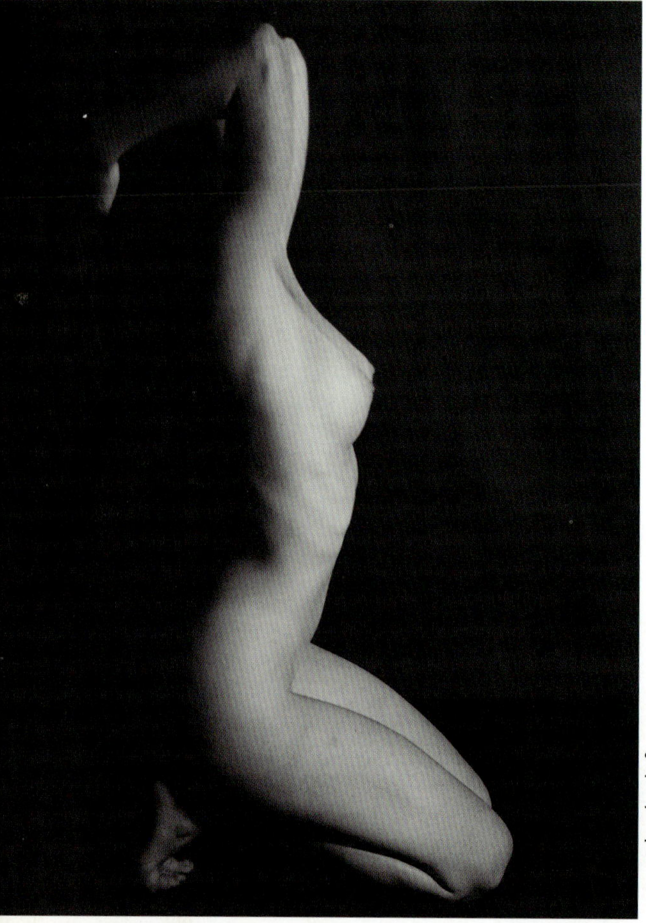

Photograph by Skip Middleton

Skip Middleton used strong directional lighting and a dark background to concentrate attention on the outline of the woman's body. He placed his flash unit about six feet in front of the model and shot from the side. He set his zoom lens at around 35mm, giving a moderately wide angle of view that suited the vertical composition.

Seeing

Here the photographer was inspired for his model's pose by the foetal position adopted by babies in the womb. The idea was to create a feeling of warmth and serenity, with the model's closed eyes suggesting security and relaxation.

Thinking

The composition is simple yet strong. Although large parts of the frame are empty, the photographer made good use of the rule of thirds. The model's body splits the frame into three roughly equal parts. There is symmetry horizontally as well as vertically: the girl's pointed foot on the left-hand side of the frame echoes her teased-out hair on the right.

Acting

The photographer positioned a softbox directly overhead to provide illumination. The foreground and background of the image were made up of a single large roll of black background paper.

Rule of Thumb

Chromogenic film is a special black and white film that is processed using chemicals normally used for colour negative films. The negatives can be used to produce colour prints although these will be monochrome, and will look as if they have been treated with a colour toning solution. Another characteristic of chromogenic films is that they have great exposure flexibility, and are usable at a wide range of different ISO speed settings.

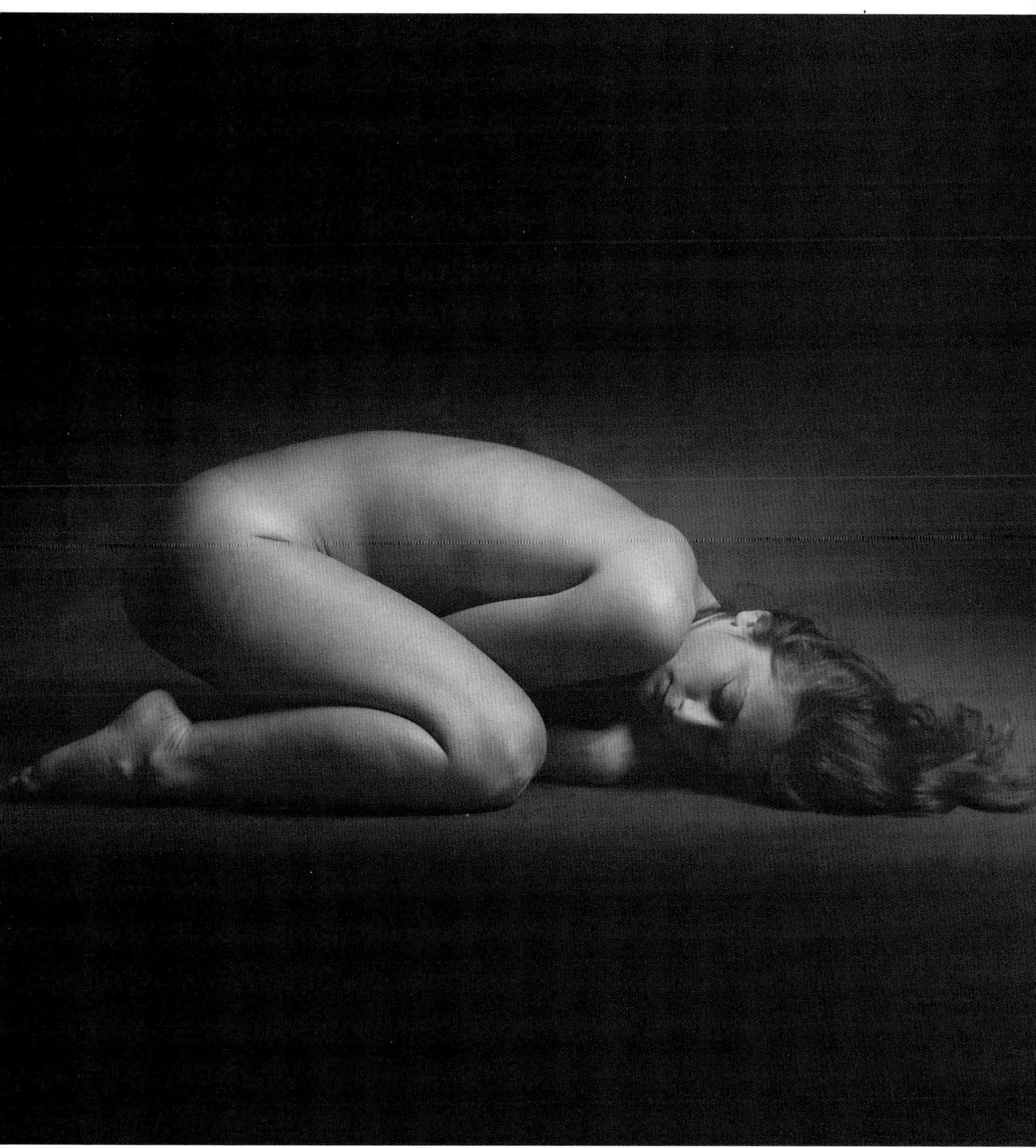

▲Technical Details

6x6cm Medium Format Camera with an 80mm standard lens and Ilford Plus-X b&w film.

Digital Effects

The power of current computer software packages means that images can be digitally manipulated even on fairly basic home computers. The world of digital effects has few limits, allowing images to be coloured, stretched or distorted in almost any way imaginable and combined with other images to create striking, eye-catching and often surreal compositions.

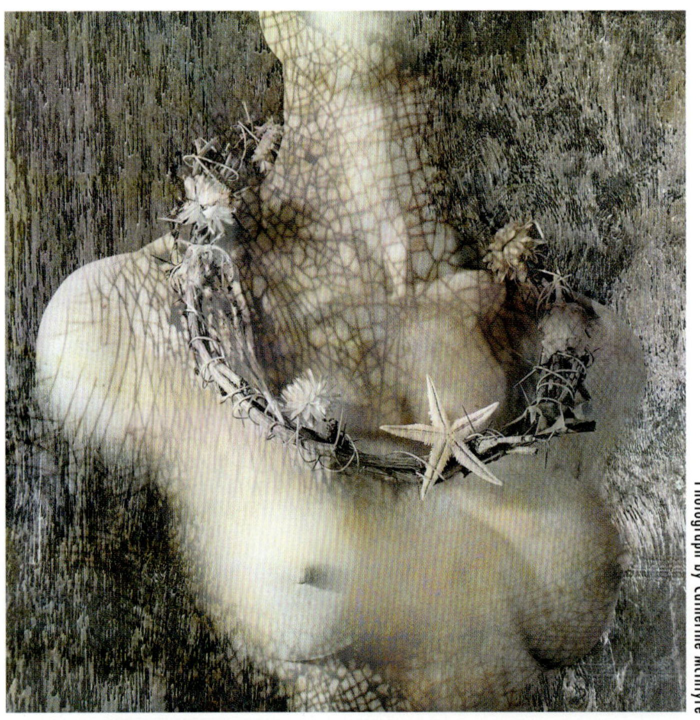

Photograph by Catherine McIntyre

With image editing software, a photograph is just the starting point for the inventive photographic illustrator. Several different elements were successfully combined in this image, which was created on a desktop computer using a popular software package.

Technical Details

Medium Format Camera with an 80mm standard lens and Agfapan 100 b&w film.

Technical Details

Medium Format Camera with an 80mm standard lens and Agfapan 100 b&w film.

Seeing

Photographer Catherine McIntyre specialises in creating digitally manipulated images. The secret of successful composite pictures lies in choosing and combining elements that complement each other. For this image she selected three elements – the nude torso, the leaf and the brocade material – that she knew would work well together.

Thinking

Flowers, leaves and other natural objects suit multiple exposures that involve the human face and body. The texture of harder objects such as rock or metal can also be used to good effect.

Acting

Having taken her image on a medium format camera and made a print, McIntyre scanned it into her desktop computer. She had earlier done the same with the leaf and the piece of brocade. Using a popular software editing package, she then overlaid the three images one on top of the other until the composition looked right. She completed the effect by digitally cutting out the image from its background, giving a bold final result.

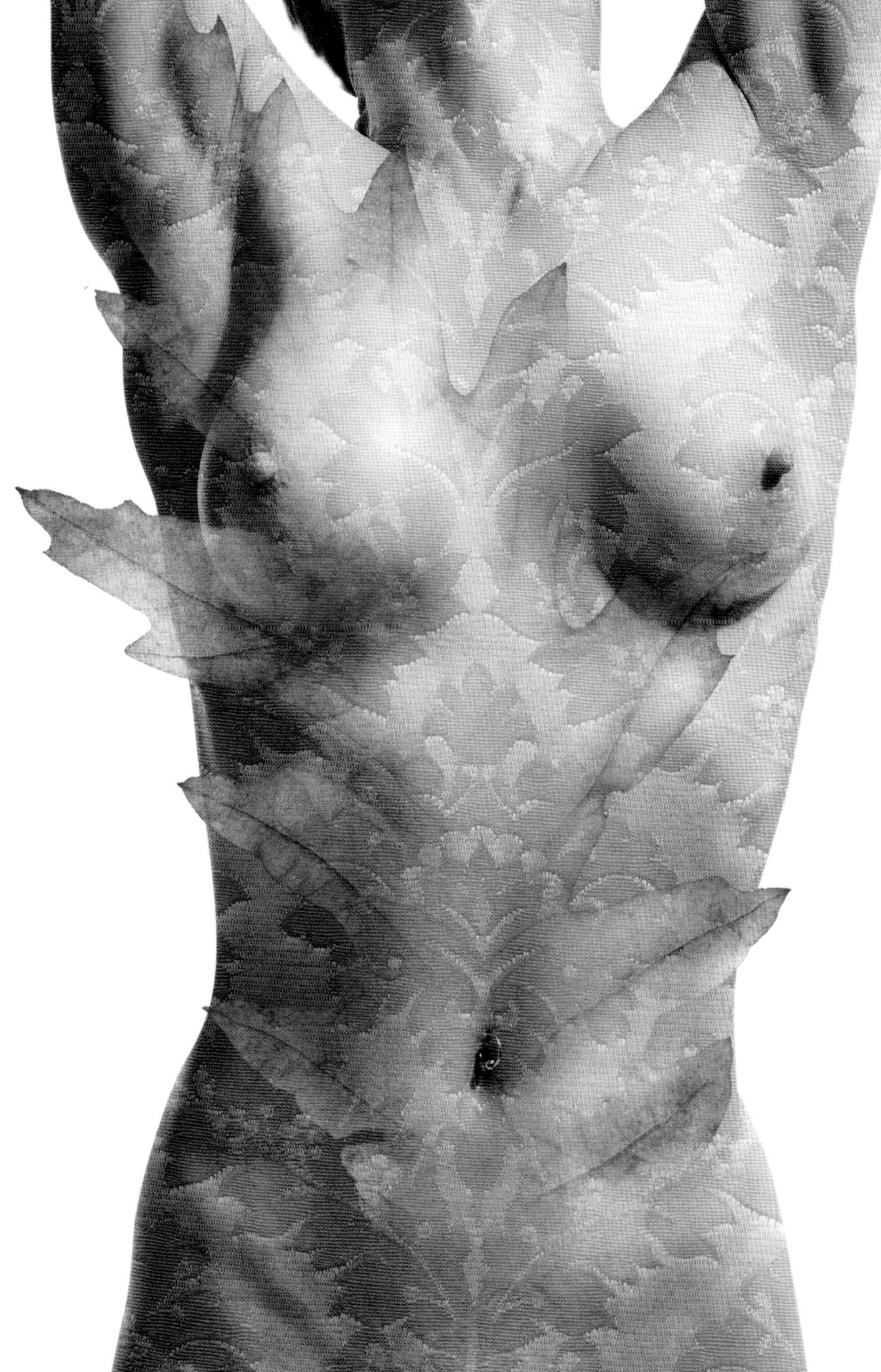

Photograph by Catherine McIntyre

Selective Illumination

Studio lighting is infinitely variable. Single lights or combinations of lights can be used to highlight selected parts of the image, picking out details and concentrating attention on elements of shape and form.

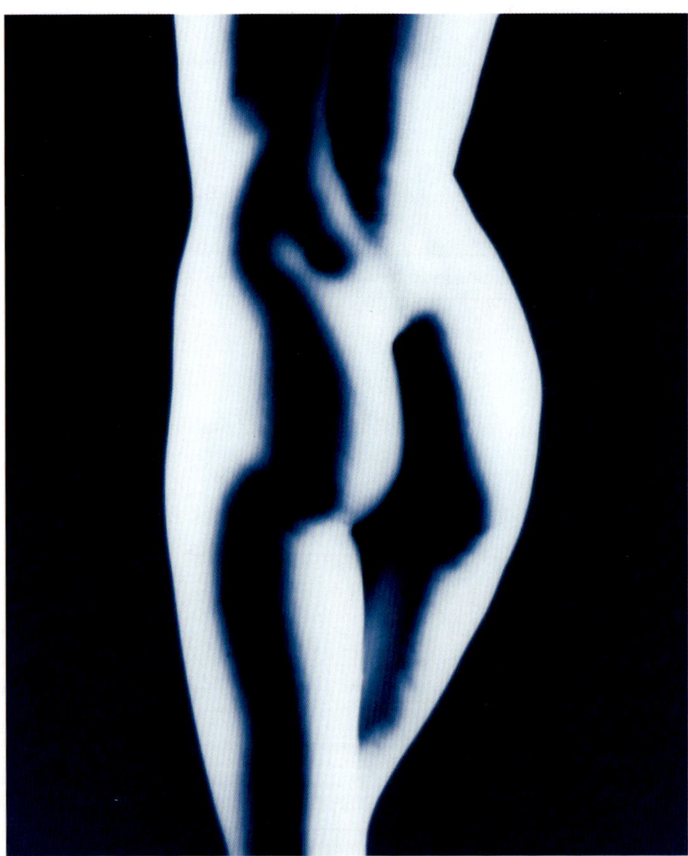

Two strong light sources were positioned to illuminate the shapes of the body in such a way that the highlighted areas dominate. The dark areas play a complementary role in defining the subject's shape and form in a strong, high-contrast manner. The original black and white print was toned blue in the darkroom.

Technical Details

35mm SLR Camera with a 35–70mm zoom lens and Kodak TMax 400 b&w film.

Seeing

Rene de Carufel wanted to create an abstract image with a soft, sensuous feel. He planned to do this by using a diffusing mask in the darkroom to soften the image, and set out to shoot the picture with this effect in mind.

Thinking

He cropped in close with a medium telephoto lens on a medium format camera to fill the frame with the curves of the model's body. He concentrated on the strong curves of her back and bottom to suggest an impression of sinuous strength.

Acting

He created the dramatic lighting effect by aiming tungsten mini spotlights at the model's shoulders and bottom. The rest of her body was lit by peripheral illumination from these two light sources. In the darkroom, printing the image through a diffusing mask gave the required soft focus effect.

Rule of Thumb

The photographer of the nude, when looking for a new approach, sometimes needs to consider the human body as an object. Many photographers approach the nude as they would a still life. Parts of the naked human body may be considered strong, simple shapes in their own right, and selective lighting can make the most of them.

Technical Details

Medium Format Camera with a 150mm telephoto lens and Kodak TMax 100 b&w film.

Photograph by Rene de Carufel

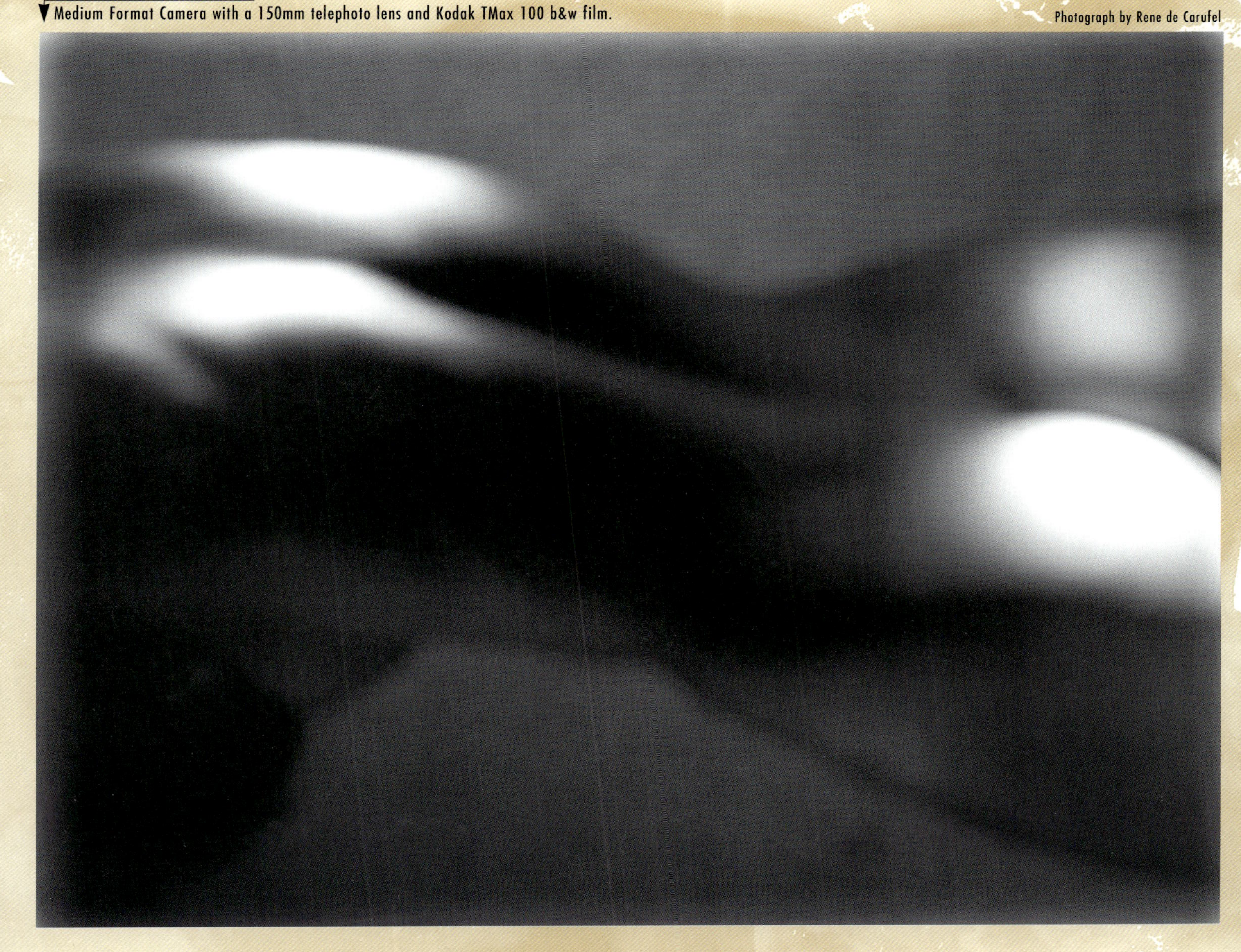

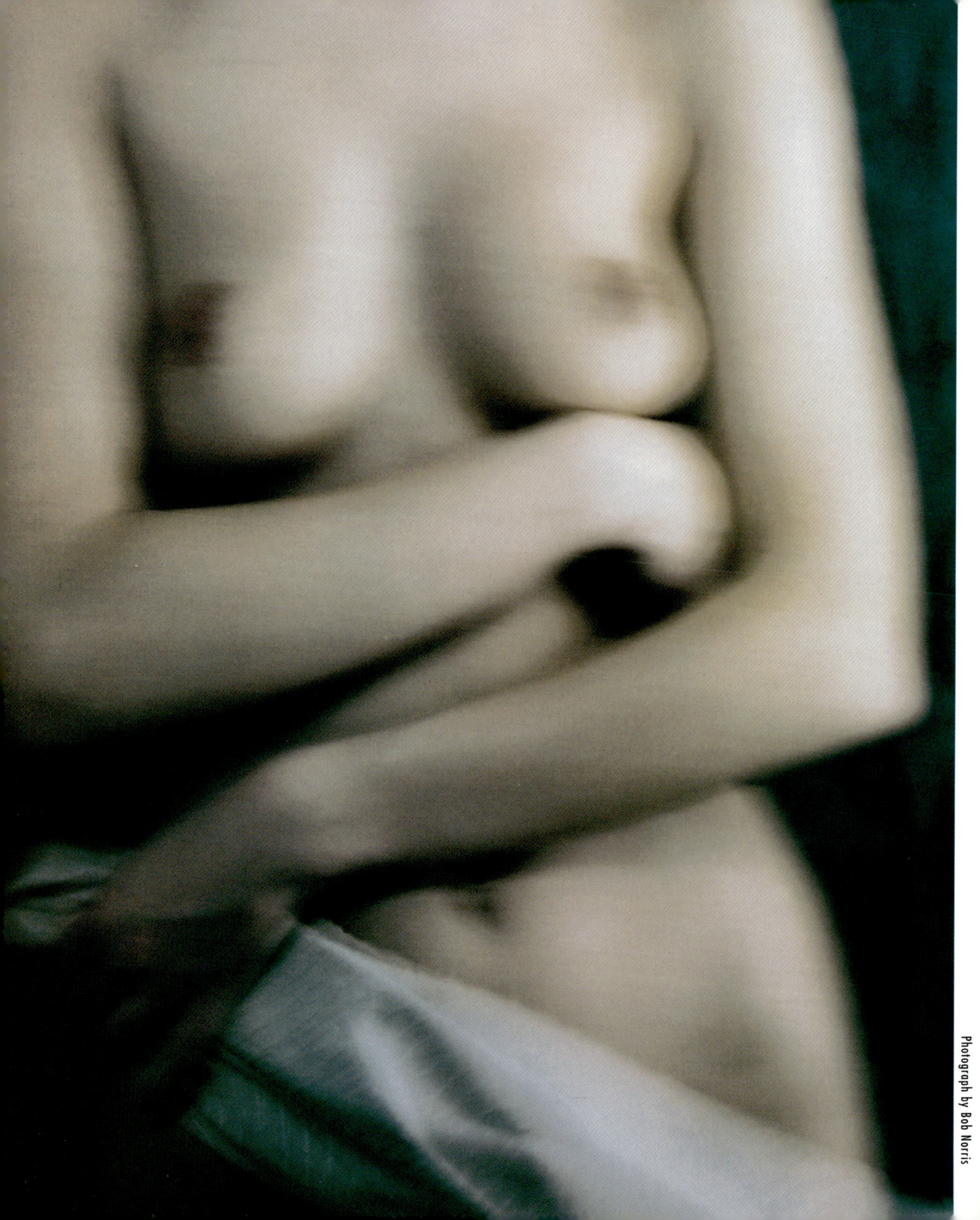

Photograph by Bob Norris

Seeing

Although it doesn't look like it, this double image was produced using only one exposure. The photographer wanted to convey a dynamic impression by capturing movement within a single frame of film.

Thinking

He used a combination of a slow shutter speed together with a burst of flash to create the effect. This is most effectively done in the studio, where the photographer has total control over the lighting set-up. He selected a studio background that would enhance the feeling of movement.

Acting

A modelling light with a fixed beam was aimed at the model. Then a flash was placed above and to her left side. The brief flash duration froze the model's movement but the shutter stayed open long enough for the film to register a 'double' image.

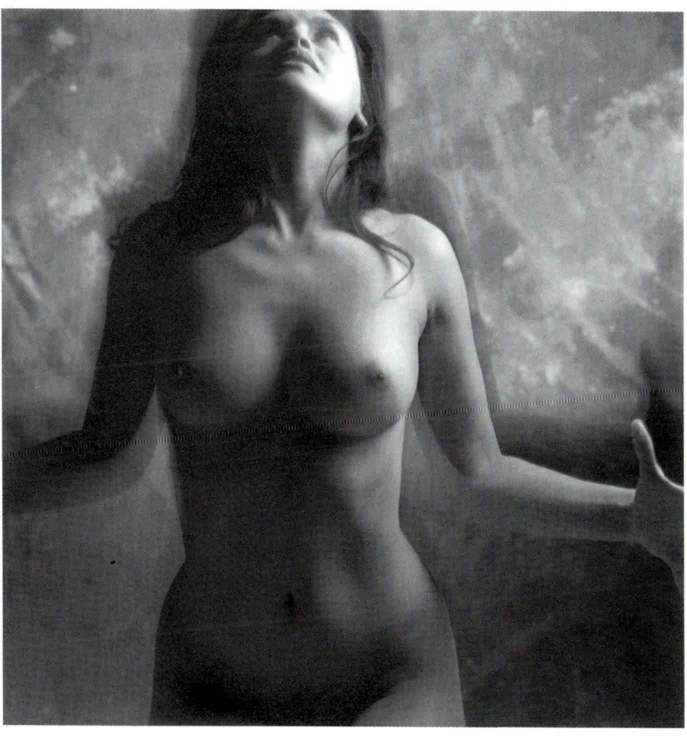

Technical Details
Medium Format Camera with a 150mm telephoto lens and Kodak TMax 100 b&w film.

Bob Norris used a two-second exposure to create the soft-focus blur in this image. The illumination came from fluorescent strip lighting which was modified by an orange filter.

Technical Details
Medium Format Camera with a telephoto lens and Polaroid 809 instant colour print film.

Silhouettes

The silhouette is a classic compositional device. The outline of the nude figure can be far more suggestive than a brightly illuminated figure that leaves nothing to the viewer's imagination. A number of different approaches can be used to create this effect.

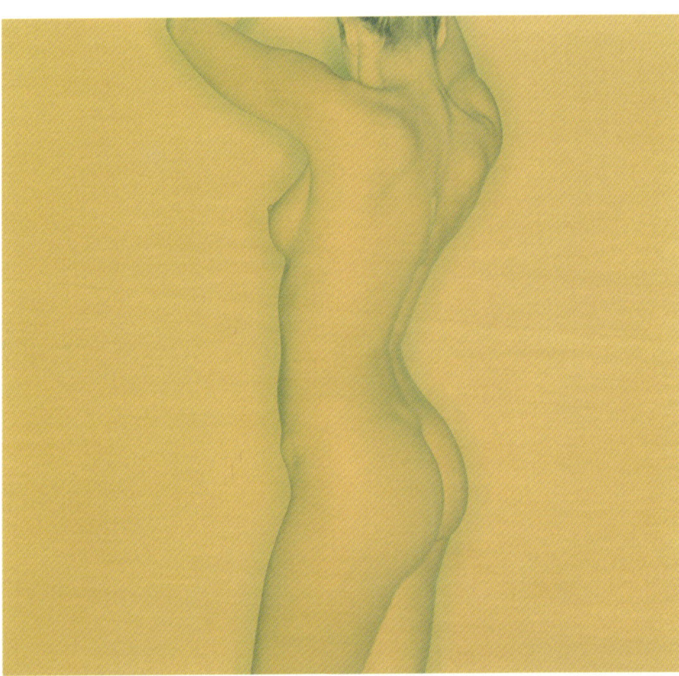

The photographer wanted to create a different type of outline here. The soft, evenly balanced lighting created by a ringflash and the positioning of the figure so close to the background created a result that is reminiscent of a drawing. The print was then toned in a special beige toning solution in the darkroom.

Seeing

The photographer set out deliberately to create a silhouette where the body is reduced to a strong, simple shape. Even in this form however it is still easy to recognise the female shape.

Thinking

This was one of a series of images pre-planned by the photographer. The outline of the model appeared softer the further away it was from the frosted perspex. The nearer she stood to the perspex, the more clearly defined her outline became.

Acting

Large light sources were aimed at the white background. The nude was placed in the foreground and the large sheet of frosted perspex was placed directly in front of her. The photographer took his exposure reading from the background rather than from the model's body. This allowed him to produce the silhouette effect.

Rule of Thumb

A ringflash is a flashgun with a circular tube which produces illumination that is almost free of shadows. It is mostly used in close-up and nature photography but more powerful types of ringflash can be used in portraiture and for nudes. It is sometimes possible to tell when a ringflash has been used by looking for ring-shaped highlights in the model's eyes or on other reflective surfaces in the picture.

Technical Details ▲
35mm SLR Camera with an 80–200mm zoom lens and Fuji Neopan b&w film.

Technical Details ►
35mm SLR Camera with a 70–210mm zoom lens and Agfa b&w film.

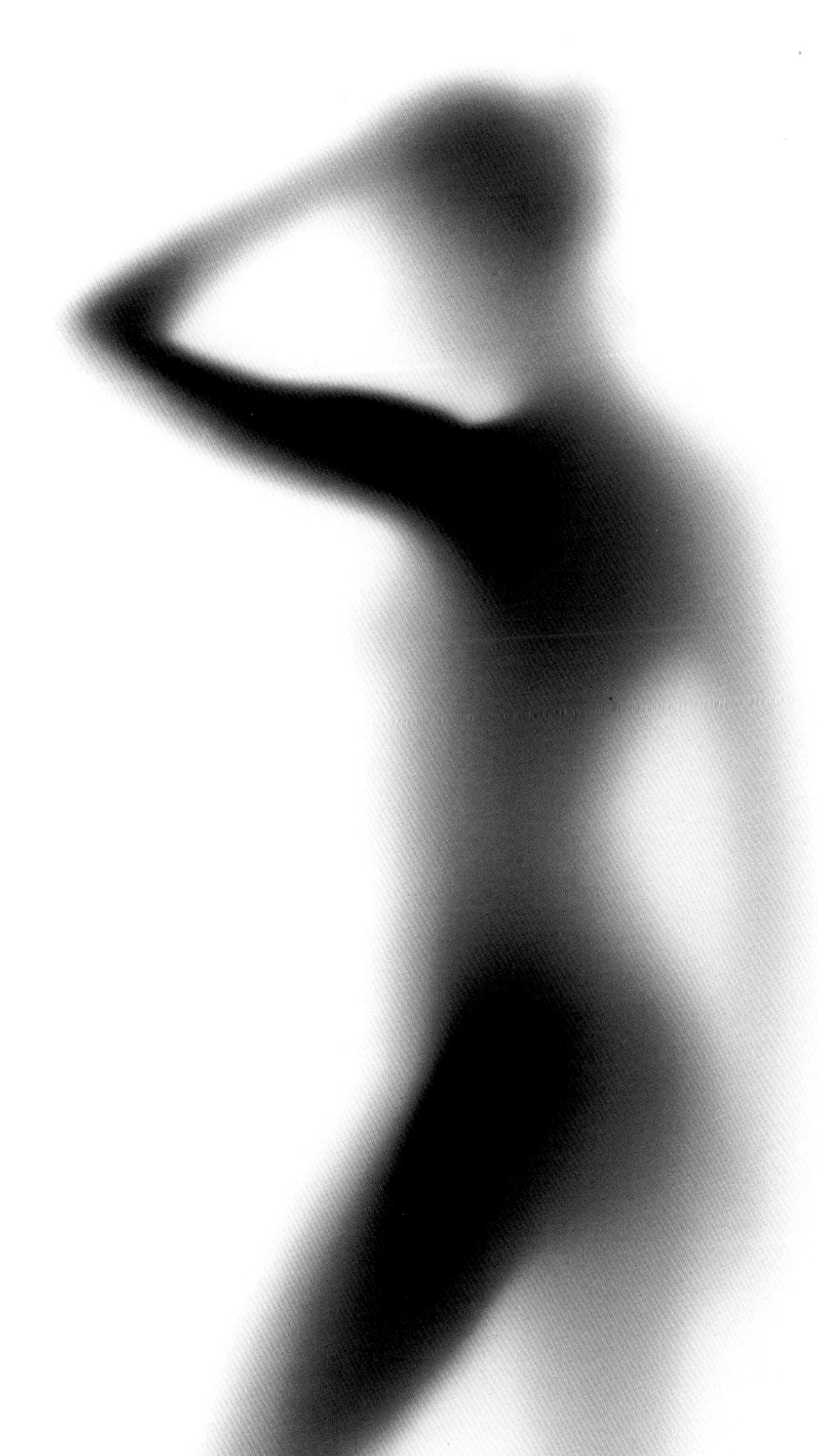

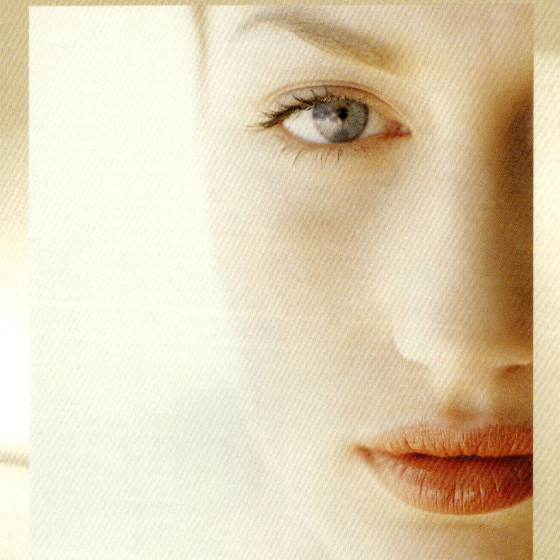

Cameras & Equipment

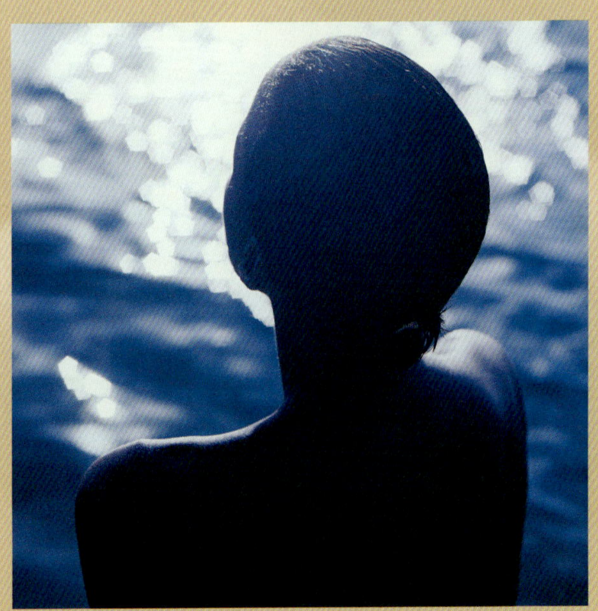

4

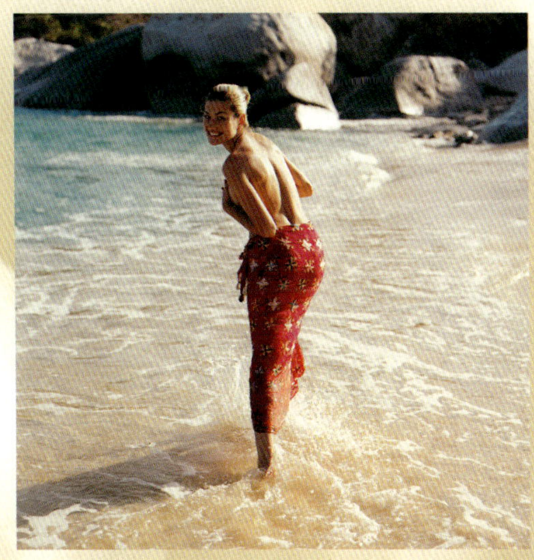

The equipment required for photographing nudes is much the same as for portrait photography but, as with portraiture, the type of nude photography undertaken will demand specific types of equipment. So the ability of a zoom lens to change the size of the image frame will be just as relevant as in portraiture, as will the camera type, film format and lighting set-up that the photographer chooses.

Choosing a Camera

A portable semi-automatic SLR camera with a zoom lens is a reasonable general choice for both outdoor and indoor nude photography. The camera is quick to use, allowing the user to make the most of changing weather and lighting conditions out of doors, while the zoom lens offers fast and convenient cropping of the image. If you require quality results plus compatibility with portable and studio flash systems, the choice is between high-end 35mm and medium format SLRs. Large format is an option for those with the necessary experience that this particular format demands, but it is not recommended for beginners.

35mm

This is the most popular film format and is used for amateur as well as professional photography. Its popularity is due to the fact that 35mm cameras are easily portable and extremely versatile. They range from snapshot cameras to single lens reflex or SLR cameras. The through-the-lens viewing capability of SLRs, showing in the viewfinder exactly what the lens 'sees', makes the system a superb aid to composition. SLRs also offer the widest interchangeability of lenses and other accessories. The range of film types available is extensive, with a variety of black and white and colour films, together with processing chemicals and paper types. However, the small frame size of 35mm film requires enlargement or magnification of the image in order to assess it accurately.

APS

Advanced Photo System or APS is a relatively new film format. It has slightly smaller dimensions than 35mm, so enabling much smaller camera types to be based around it. Commercial film processors provide index prints on which all the images on a film are printed in miniature (similar to a 35mm contact sheet). This makes it easier to select frames for enlargement. Another benefit is that APS images are easy to transfer to the digital format. A disadvantage is that, for big enlargements, the quality of APS lags behind that of the full 35mm frame.

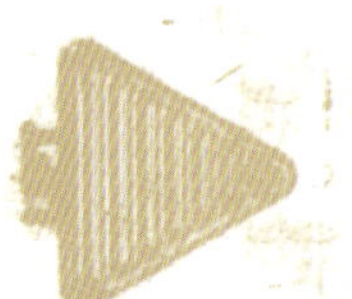

35mm is the most versatile format. 35mm cameras are small and light enough to be used hand-held, and here the photographer has made the most of that portability by following the model into the water to experiment with a variety of poses and different angles of view. The result is a picture with a spontaneous feel that would have been hard to capture if the photographer had spent a long time setting the equipment up.

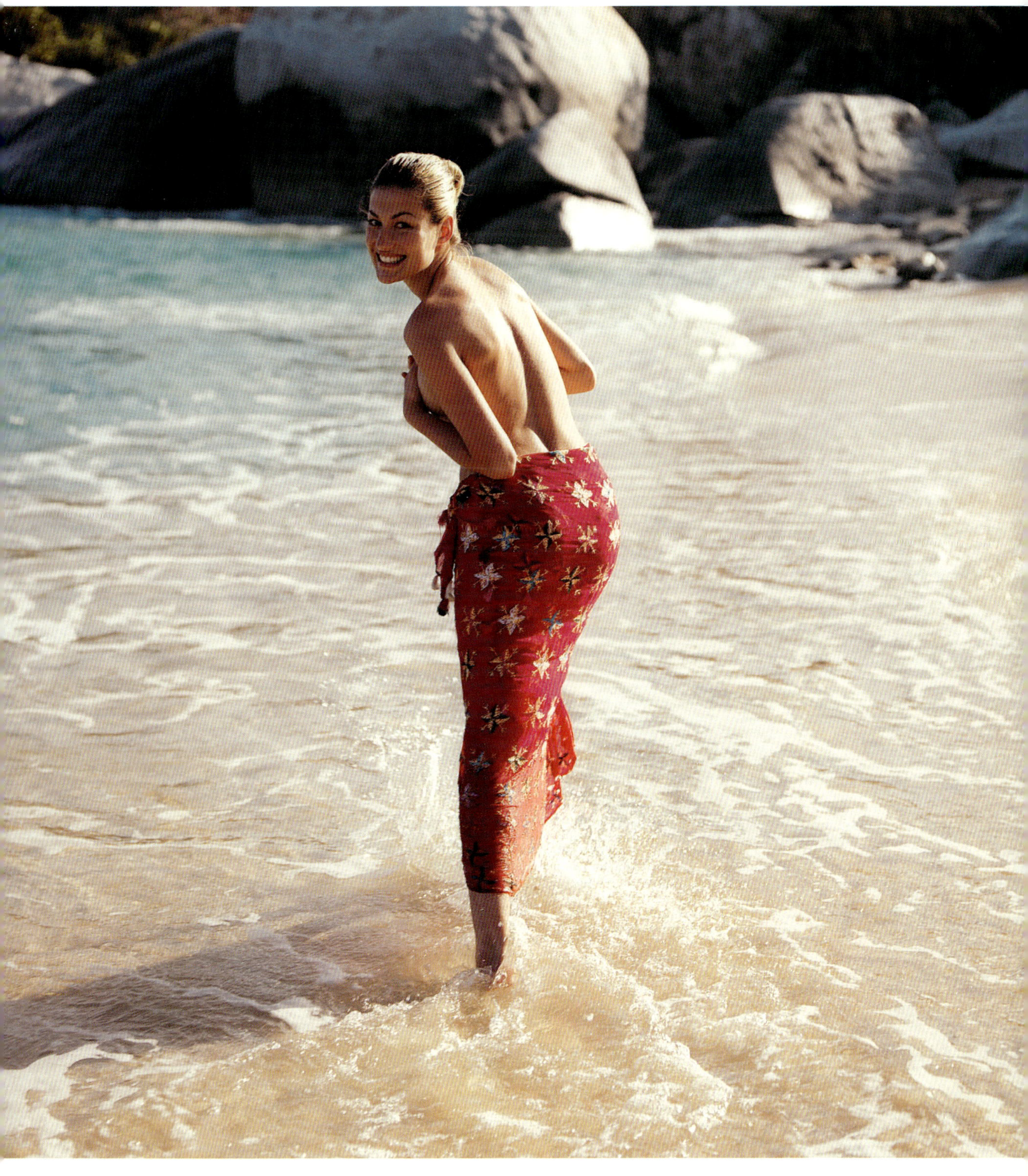

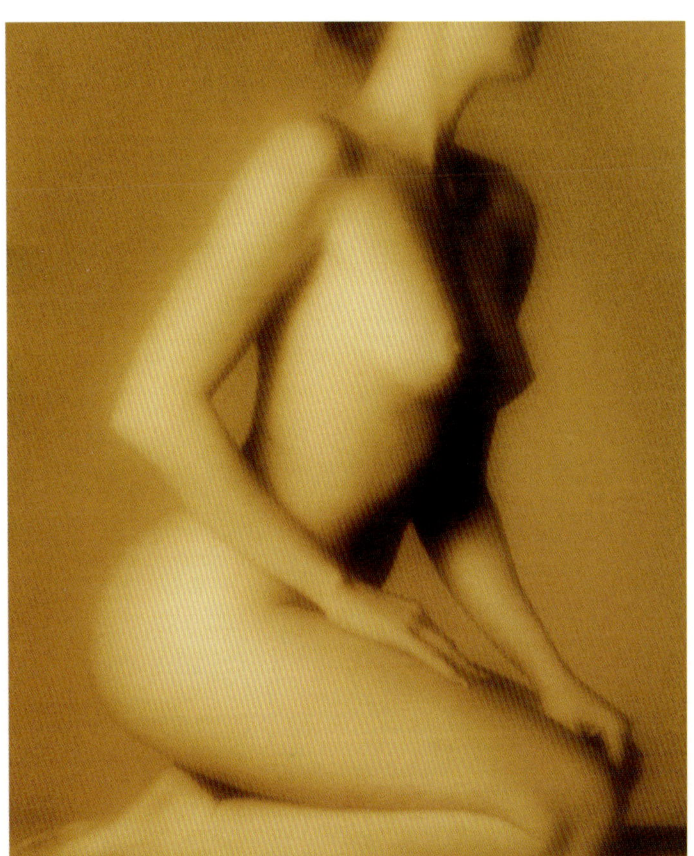

A medium format camera is a little more complicated to use than an SLR but is easier and quicker than a large format camera. However, like a large format camera, its complement of film frames (typically around 12 to 16 per roll) requires a disciplined approach to composition so as to make the most of each. Shooting sequences demands even more careful planning. Here the photographer has posed the model carefully and framed the picture precisely.

Medium format

Medium format cameras use a much larger size of film frame than 35mm. The minimum film size of 6x6cm is at least three and a half times larger. Other sizes in common use are 6x7cm and 6x9cm. There are also cameras which cater for panoramic film frame sizes such as 6x12cm and 6x17cm. The medium format film frame requires less enlargement than 35mm when making prints, and so provides a better quality image. This is most noticeable in big enlargements. The larger film size is also easier to view and assess than the smaller 35mm film frame. This is an advantage when presenting images on a commercial basis. Medium format cameras are larger and heavier than 35mm types, and often require rigid support to avoid camera shake.

Large format

Field or view cameras are also known as large format cameras. They use large format film, with typical sizes being 5x4in and 10x8in. Film frame size is one of the main attractions of this format to the serious photographer. Another is the fact that the two separate sections containing the lens/shutter unit and the film can be moved independently of each other. This provides an amazing degree of flexibility in terms of controlling the areas of sharpness in an image and the way a subject appears in the frame. View cameras tend to be used in fixed or studio locations. Field cameras are comparatively portable though they are slightly less flexible than view cameras. Both types use interchangeable film backs. This makes it easy to switch between colour, black and white or instant film.

The relative sizes of the different formats are shown here.

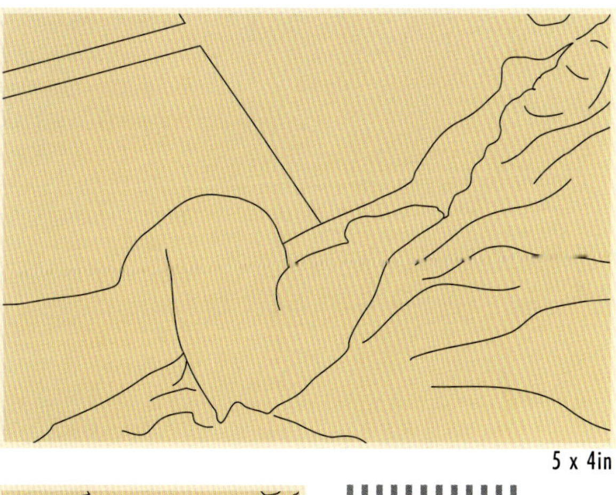

5 x 4in

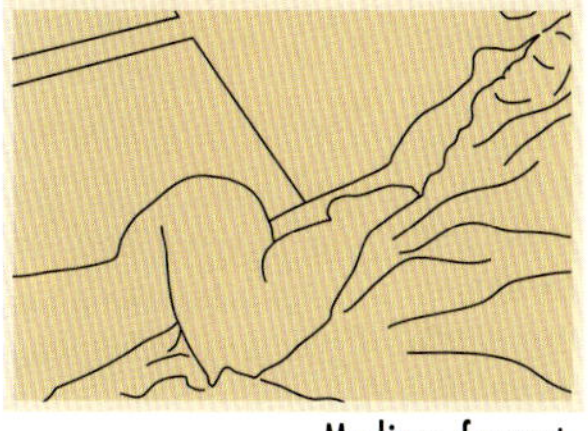

Medium format

35mm

Choosing Lenses

Choice of lens is important not just for relating lens type to specific subject areas, but also in helping a photographer to establish an identity or style. Each type of lens has its own angle of view and own special characteristics, and being aware of these gives the photographer far greater control over the range of images that can be produced.

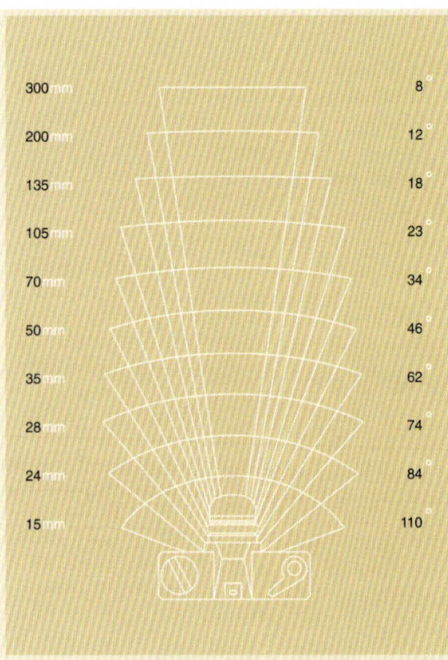

Above: These are the relative fields of view of lenses of different focal lengths in the 35mm format.

Opposite: The photographer used a telephoto lens to crop in close on part of the model's face. The telephoto lens is the nude and portrait photographer's workhorse. Its ability to flatten perspective or pick out a physical detail is useful for any kind of people photography.

35mm lenses

The 35mm format has the greatest range of accessory lens types. They can be roughly divided into fixed focal-length lenses and zoom lenses. Fixed focal-length lenses have just one focal length, the size of which relates to the lens' angle of view. The lower the figure, the wider the angle of view. 28mm is a typical focal length for a wide-angle lens. The dimensions it captures are suited to landscapes, architecture or large group portraits. There are shorter focal lengths than 28mm with dramatically wider angles of view. These reach a point where the sides of the image area bulge outward, like the sides of a barrel. A fisheye is an extreme type of wide-angle lens which produces a circular image.

50mm is a typical standard or normal focal-length lens. It is said to provide the angle of view that is closest to that of the human eye.

85mm and longer is considered to be a telephoto focal-length. Telephoto lenses have a narrower angle of view than wide-angles and give the impression of bringing distant objects closer, in a similar way to a telescope. The longer the focal length, the more pronounced the effect becomes. Popular telephoto focal-lengths are 135mm, 200mm and 300mm. There are also telephoto lenses of 500mm, 1000mm or more. Because of the way in which lenses are built, the longer the focal length, the larger and heavier the lens becomes.

In the longest focal-length ranges there are alternatives to conventional telephotos. These are called mirror lenses because they contain mirrors that shorten the distance between the front element of the lens and the film plane in the camera. Their design enables them to cover the same focal-length range as conventional telephotos but with a much more compact lens barrel.

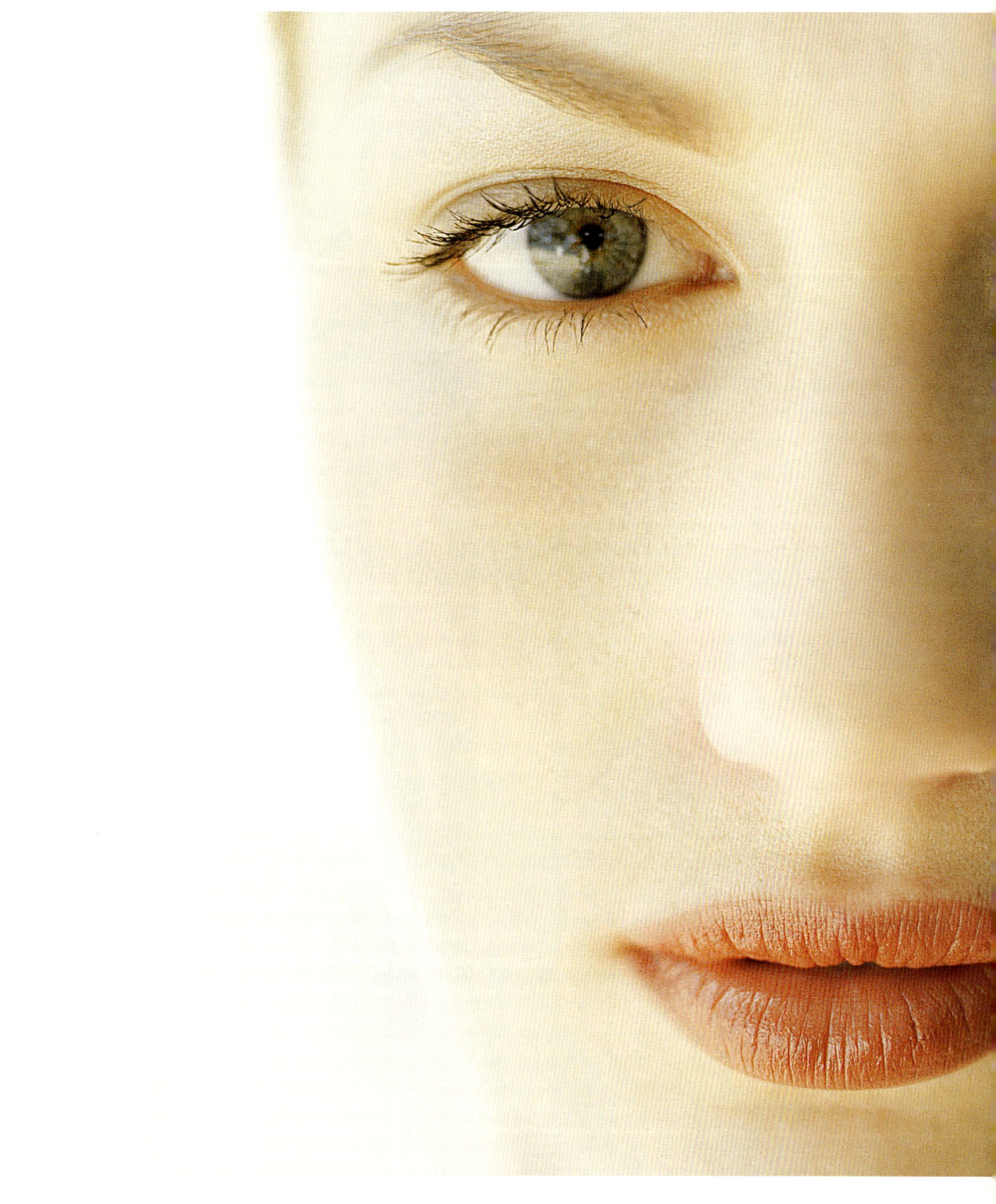

35mm zoom lenses

A zoom lens has different focal lengths within its range, and so it does the job of several lenses. Popular zoom focal-length ranges are 28–70mm, 35–70mm, 70–210mm and 80–200mm. There are numerous other zooms that go beyond the limits of these focal lengths.

The maximum or widest aperture setting of a zoom lens is usually smaller than that of a fixed focal-length lens. The average widest aperture of a 35–70mm zoom is f3.5, while a common maximum aperture for a fixed focal length 35mm lens is f2.8. Typically, the widest aperture of an 85mm lens and the most popular lens for portraits is also f2.8.

For most picture-taking situations this is not a serious limitation. The sheer flexibility offered by a zoom lens more than compensates for the slight restriction in maximum aperture.

Medium format lenses

Because the focal lengths of lenses relate to the size of the film frame being used, lenses for medium format cameras are classified differently from lenses for 35mm cameras. With the 6x6cm format, for example, a standard lens is 80mm instead of 50mm, while a good portrait lens length is 150mm. Anything below around 70mm is a wide-angle. Zoom lenses are also available for medium format cameras.

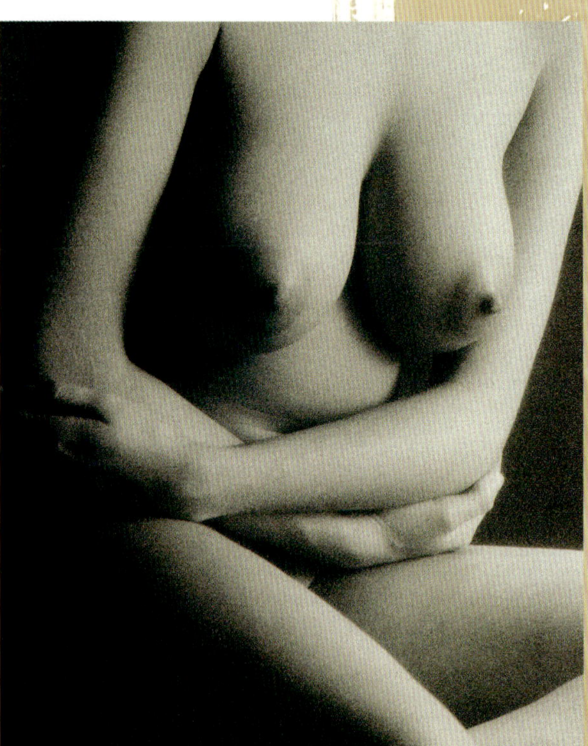

In a confined space, zoom enables versatile adjustments of image frame without the photographer having to shift position. This image was taken at the 70mm setting on a 70–210mm zoom lens.

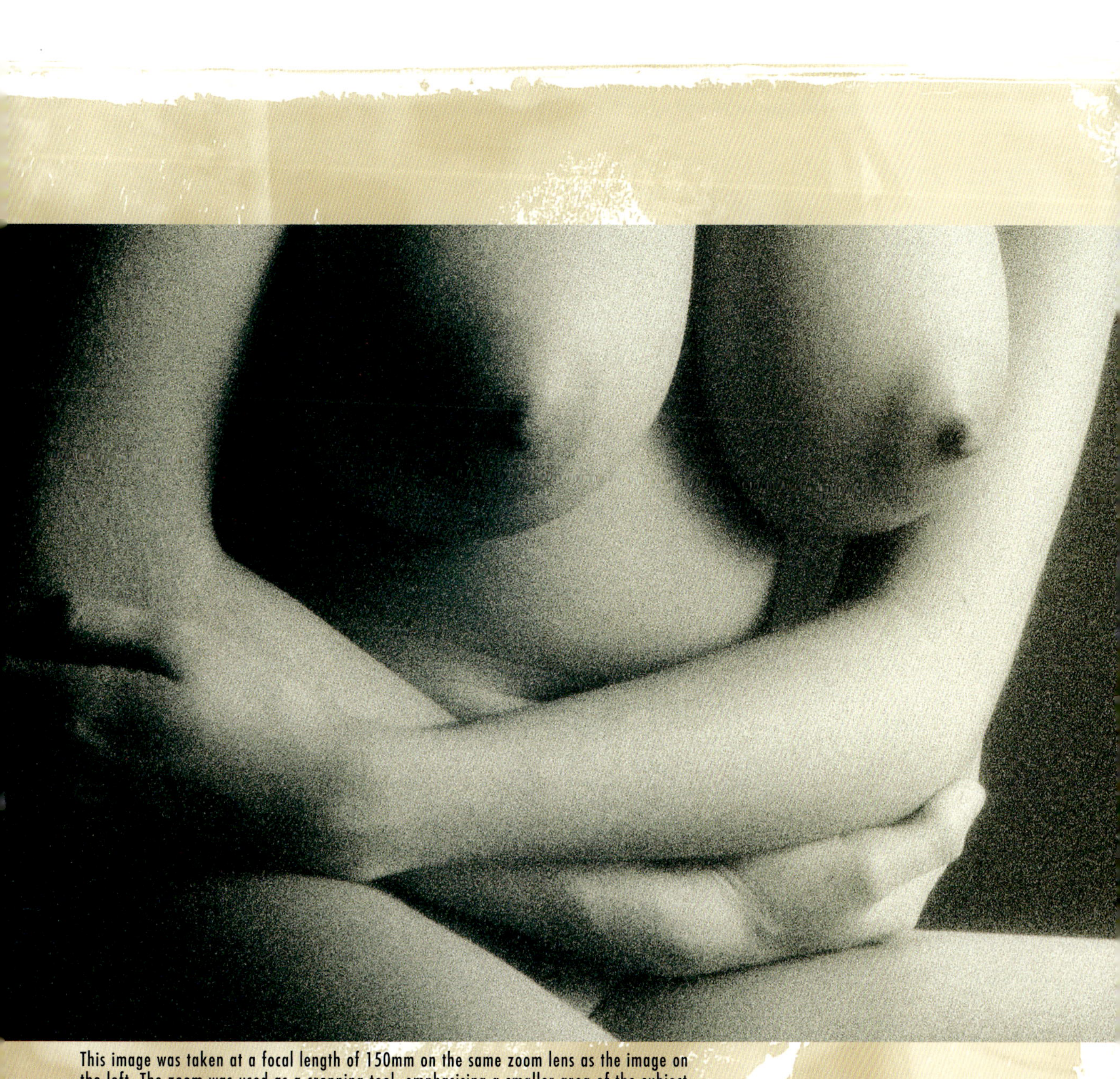

This image was taken at a focal length of 150mm on the same zoom lens as the image on the left. The zoom was used as a cropping tool, emphasising a smaller area of the subject.

Understanding Exposure

Exposure is the cornerstone of all photography. The amount of light entering the lens and striking the film, and the length of time for which it does so, are the two most crucial factors in determining the image that is recorded. Although modern cameras with their automatic exposure systems are capable of producing acceptable images most of the time, the creative photographer will want to take far greater control of the exposure process.

In most cameras, built-in exposure systems are very sensitive and can cope with the majority of available light situations. Nearly all also provide fully manual exposure options, giving the photographer more direct creative control over exposure.

Even the smallest exposure adjustments can make a strong difference to an image. An increase or decrease in exposure can have a lightening or darkening effect and so completely change the mood of the photograph. This effect is of course more pronounced with more extreme exposure adjustments.

Once the image has been sharply focused, different apertures will have an effect on the areas of sharpness within it. A wide aperture produces a narrow band of sharpness, making areas that are not within this range appear soft and out of focus. This result, known as differential focus, can be highly effective when deliberately emphasised.

A small aperture ensures that more areas within the image fall within the zone of sharpness. This setting is used most often in landscape photography, but it also has benefits in nude photography and portraiture.

Apertures are described by f stop numbers, which on most lenses are inscribed on the lens barrel. They usually run from around f2 to f32, although not all lenses cover the full range. The higher the f stop number the smaller the aperture so, for example, f2.8 is a large aperture while f16 is a small one. Each increase in aperture doubles the amount of light entering the lens while each decrease in aperture halves it. Therefore an aperture of, say, f4 gives twice the exposure of f5.6, the next stop down.

A change of shutter speed can also have a strong effect on an image. A moving subject when photographed using a fast shutter speed will appear frozen. The same subject, when photographed using a slow shutter speed, will appear as a blur.

Even the most sophisticated metering system is capable of errors in tricky lighting conditions. Exposure compensation is a crucial feature on the camera, giving the option of overriding automated exposure settings to produce a balanced result. Here the photographer had to contend with very strong backlighting from the sunlight bouncing off the water, and so opened the lens up a little to record some detail in the model's shoulders.

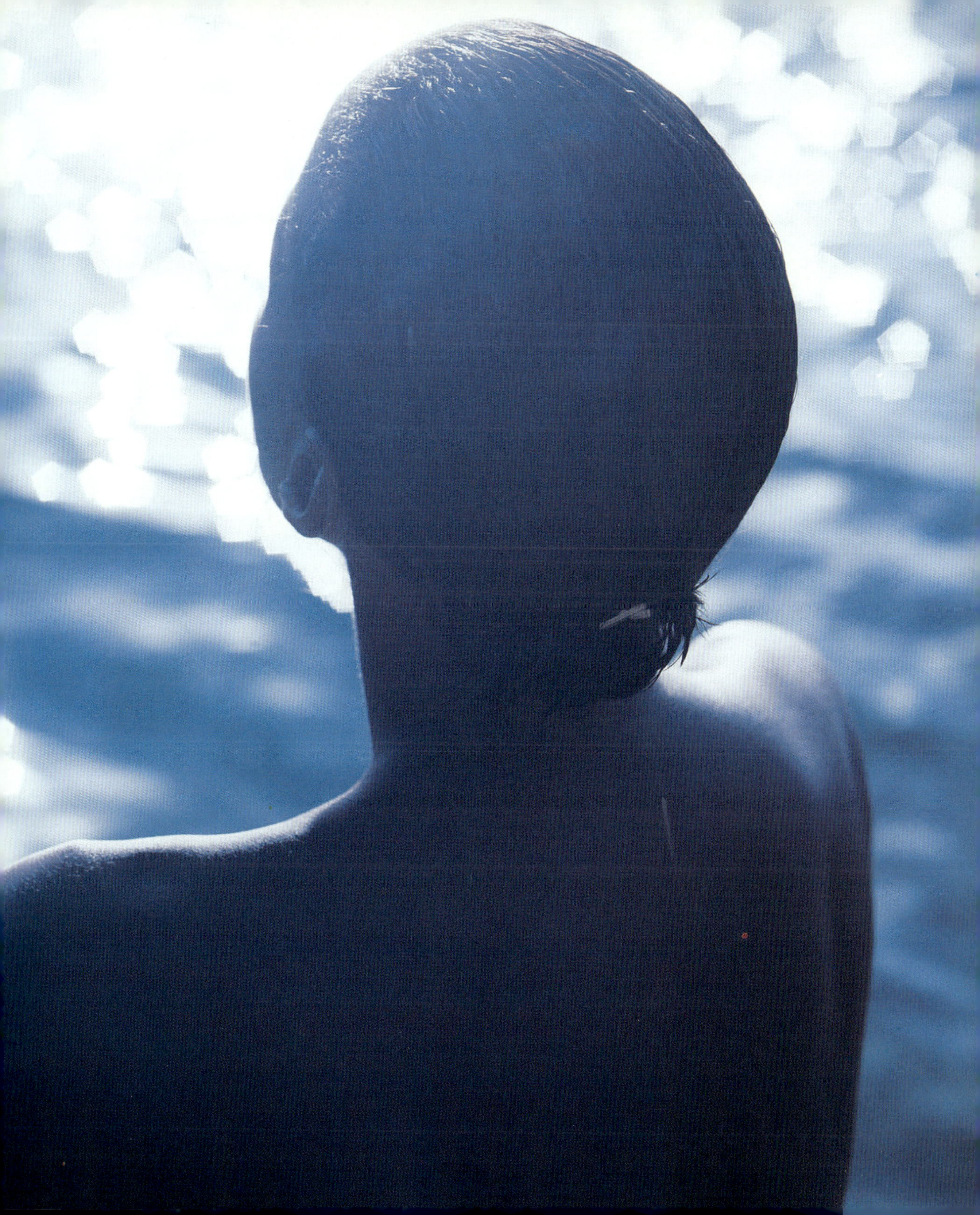

Lighting Equipment

Lighting accessories range from a plain sheet of white card used as a reflector to sophisticated arrays of studio flashguns and spotlights. Even the simplest equipment can greatly extend the range of picture-taking possibilities.

Flash

Many 35mm cameras, whether compact or SLR, have built-in flash. These built-in units are rarely powerful enough for full-length portraits but they may suffice in an emergency or for detail shots.

A more powerful alternative is an accessory flashgun. These come in a wide range of power outputs and features. Some of the top-level flashguns have similar performance to that of low-end studio flash units.

Studio lighting

Studio flash is the most powerful and versatile source of artificial illumination, giving the photographer comprehensive control over lighting. A modest selection of equipment hugely increases the range of possibilities.

Photo-flood, or tungsten halogen, lamps are the mainstay of the studio photographer. They can be used as straightforward illumination or their light can be modified. A piece of frosted acetate, a sheet of tracing paper or a length of fabric such as muslin are all items that can be used to diffuse the light for a softer effect, while light spill can be controlled by attaching accessories such as spotlights, barn doors or snoots.

It is important to pay attention to backgrounds. These can be bought ready-made, in the shape of wide rolls of cartridge paper which are available from specialist photo stores and come in a wide variety of colours, or you can create your own, using fabrics such as velvet and silk.

Reflectors

One of the simplest yet most effective lighting accessories is a reflector. In available lighting, a reflective object such as a piece of white card or a pale-coloured wall can have a considerable effect on the final result. Purpose-made reflectors, filling in shadow areas or creating high-key lighting effects, can transform an image. Reflectors used with flash can even be used to make subtle colour adjustments.

A softbox

A softbox is an extremely popular type of reflector. It is basically a white umbrella-type reflector covered with a translucent screen which diffuses the light and gives a pleasingly soft lighting effect.

A reflector bounces light back towards a subject. Here a gold-coloured reflector has produced a warm result that enhances the subject's skin tones.

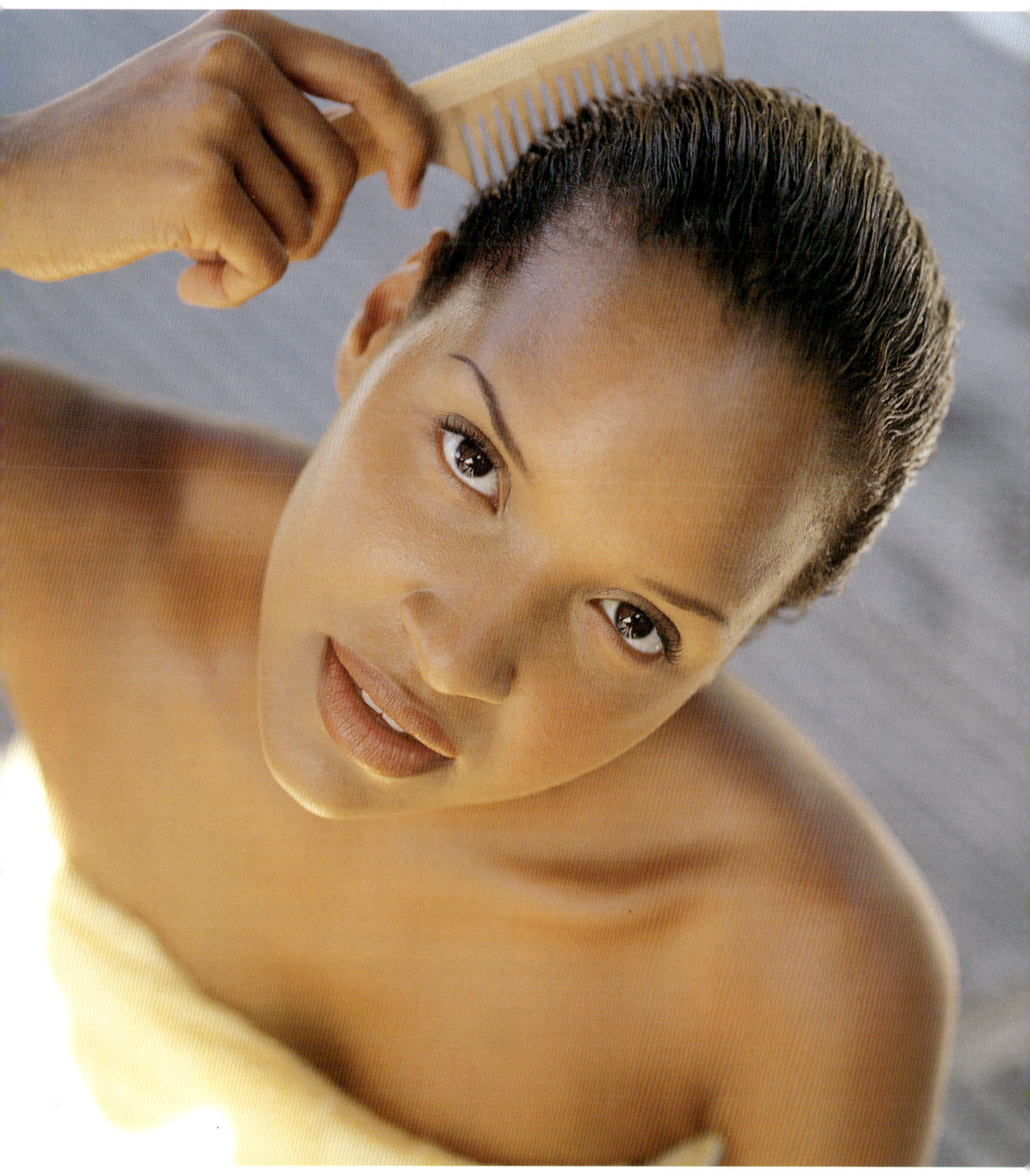

Choosing Film

Film is the raw material of photography. There are many different types of film available, each with its own set of characteristics that will influence the look and feel of the finished image.

Film

The main choice when it comes to film is between colour and black and white, although there are different types of each. Colour film encompasses colour prints and colour transparencies, as well as instant colour prints which are generally used as a reference guide when setting up a shot. Black and white films usually produce a negative from which a print is made, although black and white transparency films do exist. Chromogenic film is a black and white film designed to be developed in colour chemicals, which has a wide exposure latitude.

Within these different film categories there are slow, medium and fast ISO speed films. Slow films tend to be sharper and have a better tonal range than faster films. Some very high ISO speed films have a noticeably grainy appearance which many consider an appealing visual effect.

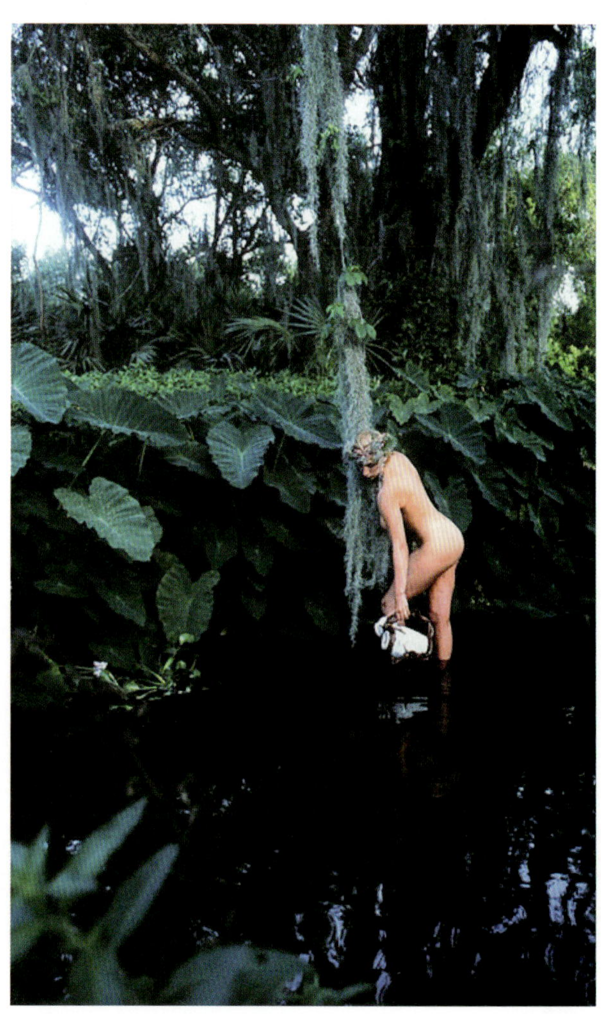

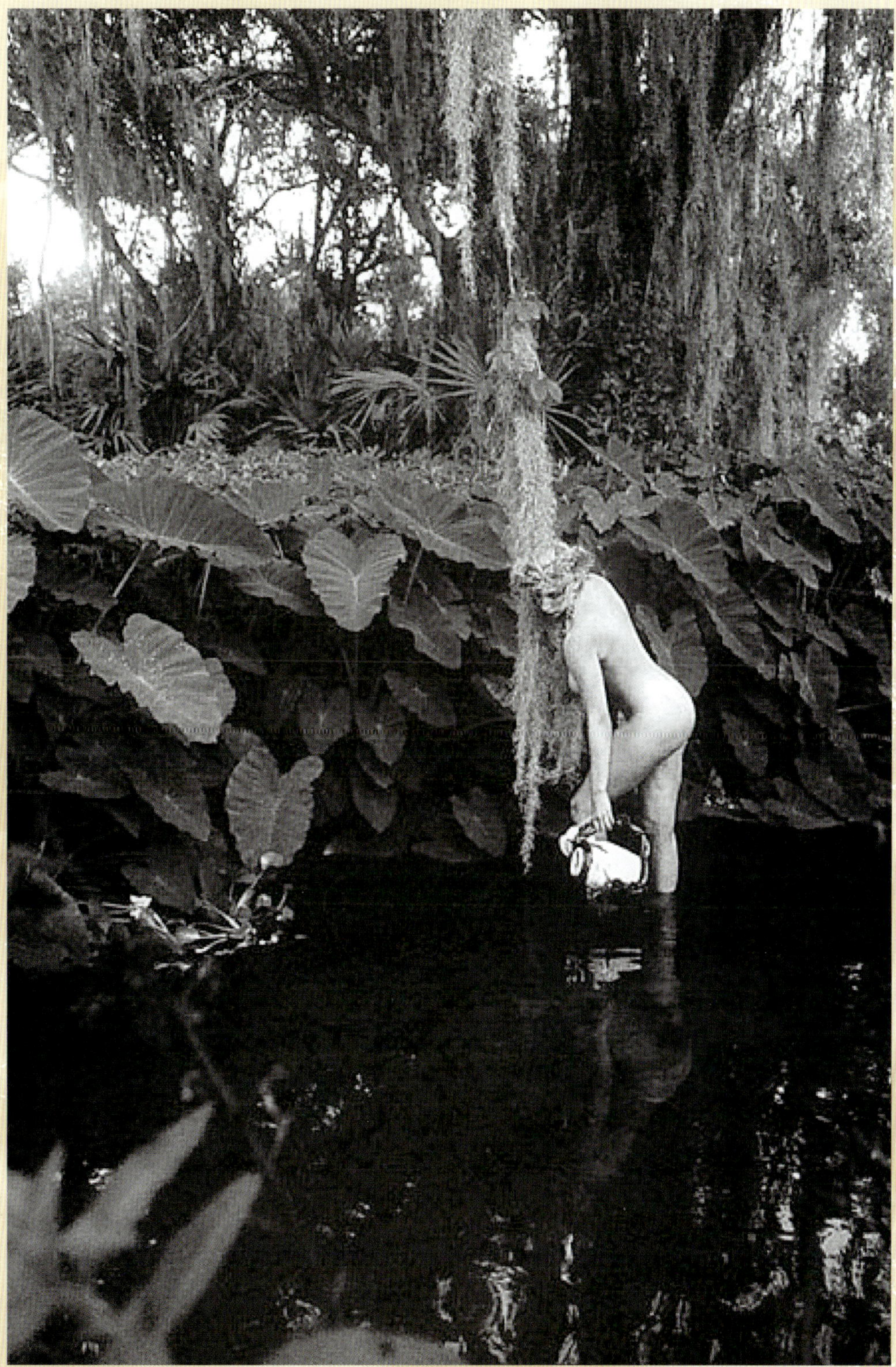

Black and white or colour? Black and white places emphasis on shape, contrast and tonal values. The photographer tried out both during the same shooting session and the differences are very striking. Colour is altogether brighter, deriving much of its impact from the effects of complementary or contrasting colours used in combination with one another. Both colour and black and white have their adherents: some argue that colour has more impact, while others feel that the subtlety of black and white is more rewarding. Decide for yourself – but try both!

Using Filters

Special effects filters can have a dramatic effect on an image though, as in any type of photography, they should be used sparingly. For nude photography, however, a small selection of warm-up and colour compensation filters is a useful addition to any photographer's gadget bag.

A filter is an inexpensive accessory that can have a dramatic effect on a photograph. Filters come in a variety of types. Two that photographers of nudes may find useful are warming filters and colour compensation filters. Warming filters are generally pale orange or pale pink in appearance. They give a warm appearance to skin tones, and are used to compensate for the faint blue-ish tinge that can occur in daylight.

Colour compensation filters have a more extreme effect, and are used to combat some of the effects that artificial lighting has on normal (or daylight balanced) film. Ordinary room lighting, for instance, results in photographs with a strong yellow-orange colouring. A blue filter will reduce the effect of the lighting and make the colours appear more natural.

Fluorescent or strip lighting often produces a greenish tinge. Using a pink or a mauve filter will compensate for this.

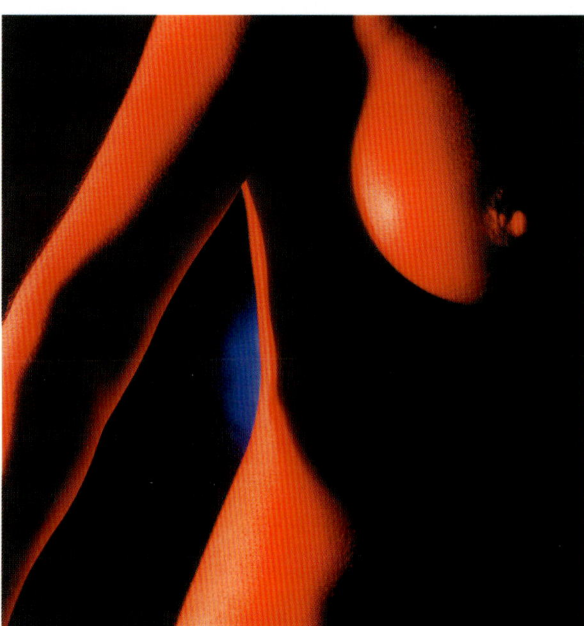

A filter placed over a camera lens provides one effect at a time. But filters used on different artificial light sources – such as the red and blue gels used in these shots – give the option of including several effects in a single image. More subtle colour effects are also possible, as numerous filter and gel colours are available – and you can even make your own.

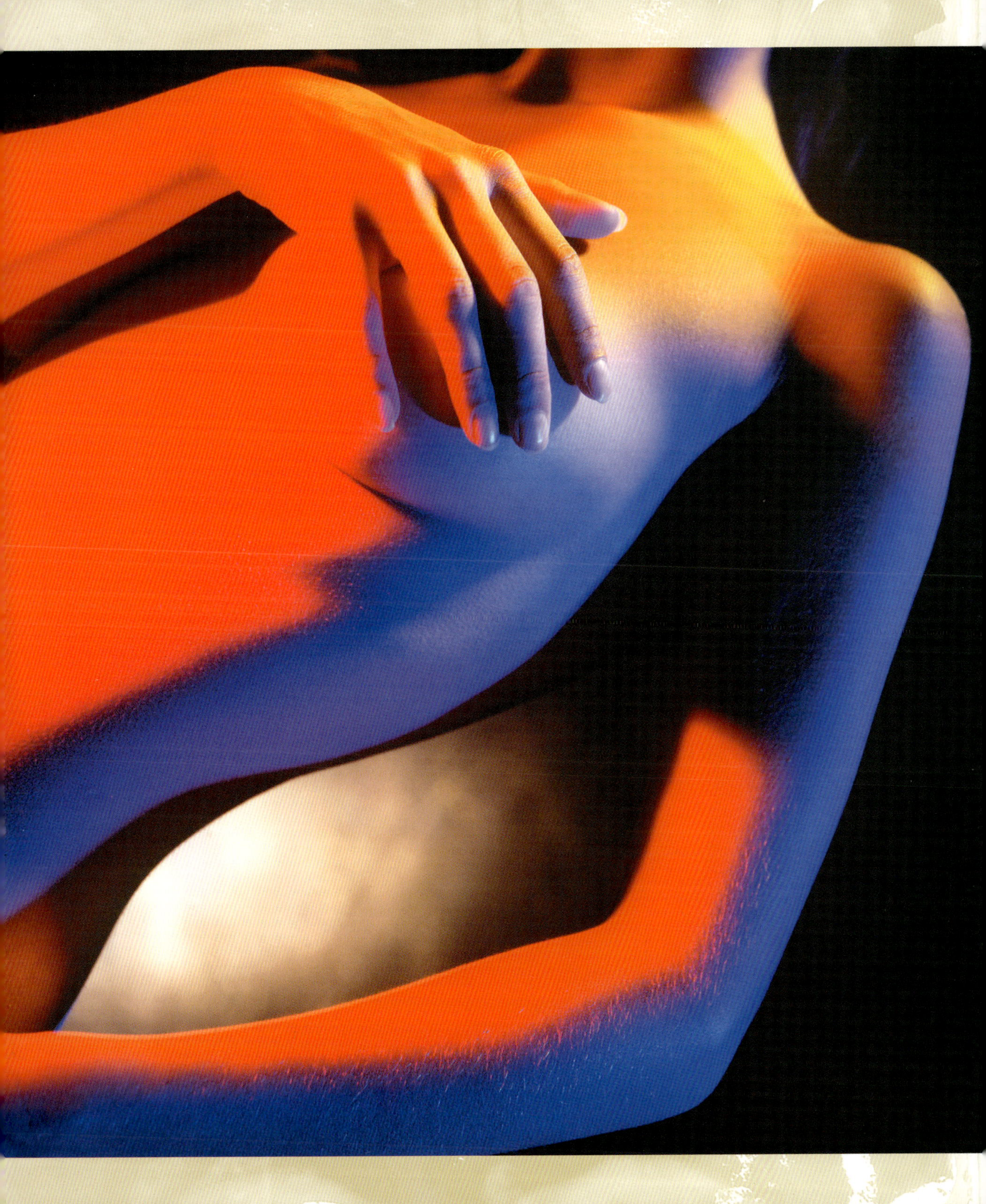

Storing, Finishing & Presentation

Beautiful images deserve careful storage and thoughtful presentation. The way an image is framed and mounted can make all the difference to the way it is perceived. This is an important consideration for any photographer with ambitions to display their work, whether simply for the enjoyment of friends and family or for a wider audience.

Selecting

Only choose your best images, never those that were nearly the best, even if it means that your selection of images is drastically reduced. This way you will always feel confident that your very best quality images are on display. Mediocre images are a distraction and can dilute the combined visual effect of a display of high quality photographs.

Storing

Transparencies are best stored in plastic sleeves, preferably with an additional protective plastic cover. Negatives are best stored in glassine or paper sleeves. Specially made archival plastic and paper sleeves are so called because they don't contain acids that emit chemical fumes. These may affect the film or print surface over extended periods. There is also special archival card that is used for framing prints, and acid-free adhesive material.

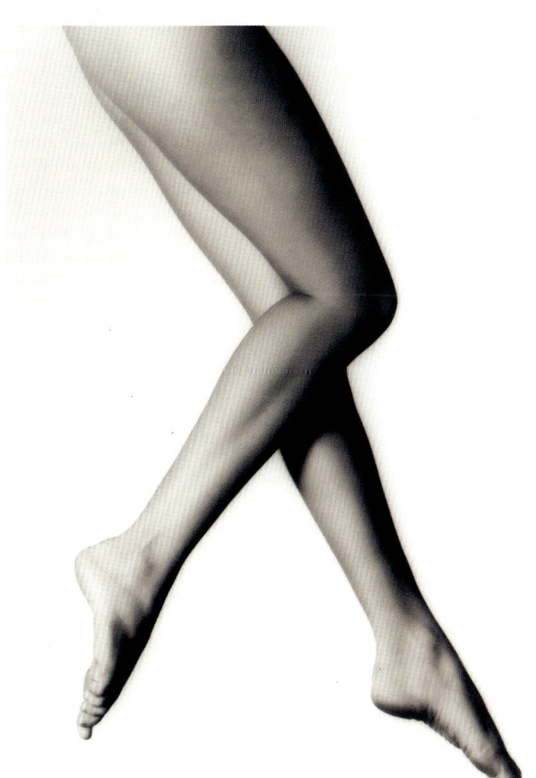

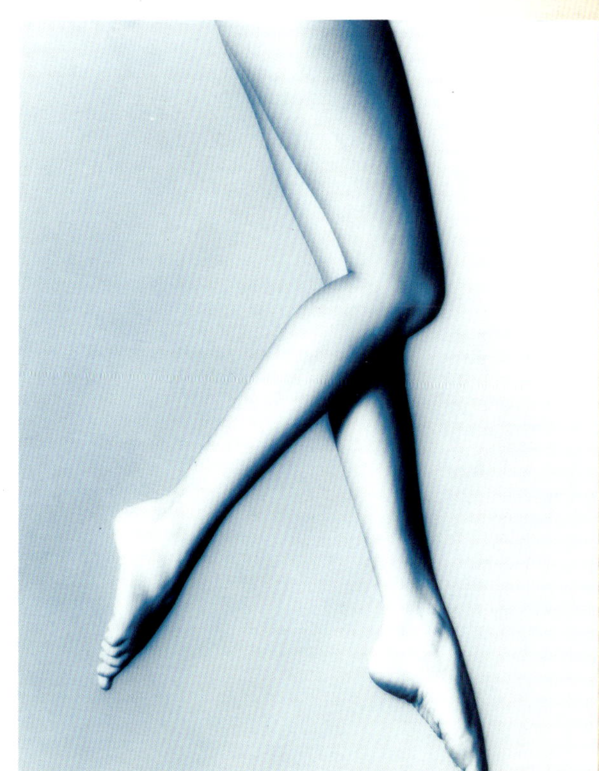

Grouping similar subject areas together provides a visual change of pace when displaying images. In some cases, particularly with abstract compositions, repeating the image or juxtaposing variations of the same image can have a strong impact.

Displaying

The way an image is displayed, either projected as a transparency or as a print placed in a framed mount, will determine the impact it has on the viewer. Transparencies can be presented in a sleeve with pockets or, for more impact, in special black card mounts which have small windows for each image.

Transparencies are most effectively displayed via a slide projector which shows them as enlarged images. With prints there is a vital relationship between the size of the image itself and the dimensions of the frame that surrounds it. The colour of the frame also plays an important role, complementing or contrasting with the colours in the image itself. For this reason it is worth taking the time to ensure that the frame you select displays the image to its best advantage.

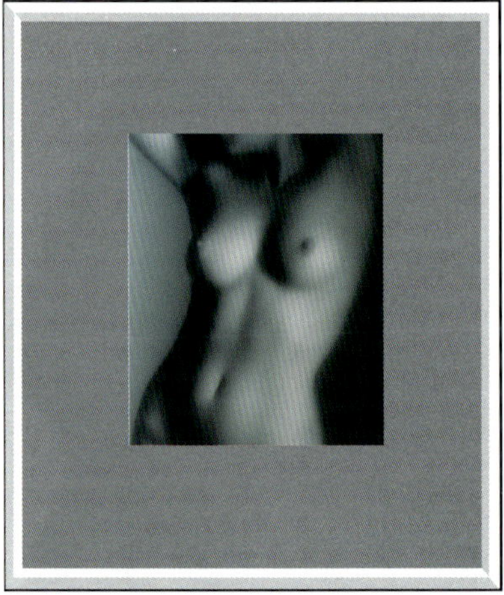

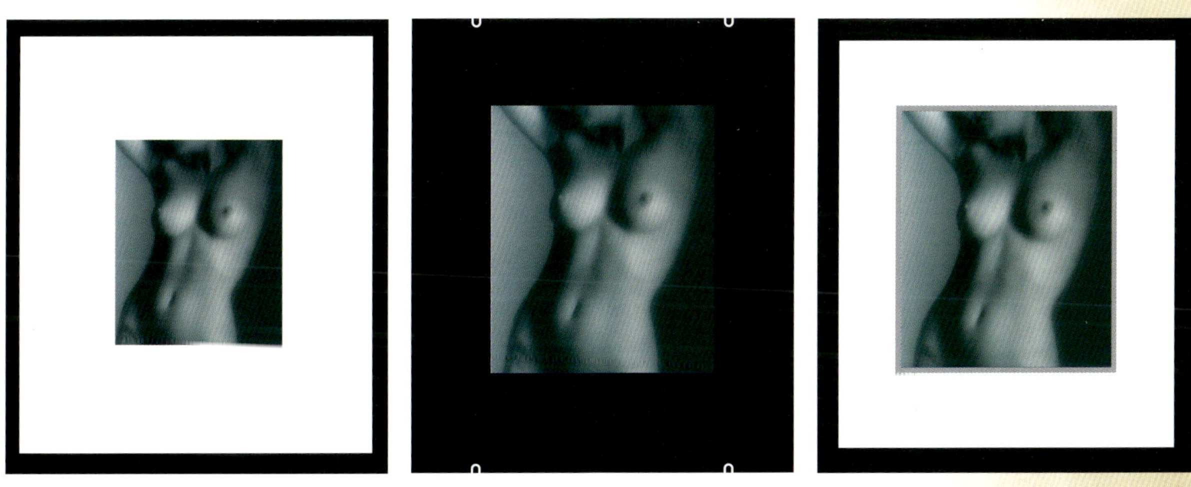

Different frame types and sizes have a subtle effect on the impact of a photograph. Notice how different frame widths and colours affect the presentation of the image.

Glossary

AF assist
A feature of an autofocus flashgun that projects an infrared beam on to a subject. The camera's autofocus system will recognise this and lock on to it, to achieve a sharply focused image. It's a useful feature when photographing in low light. Autofocus systems use contrast as a basis for focusing. The image projected by the AF assist flash is a high-contrast pattern that is a perfect target.

AE lock
Auto-exposure lock is a widely used feature found in automatic exposure cameras. It's used to temporarily memorise a particular exposure setting.

Air release
This is a cable release that is operated by air pumped by a rubber bulb. It produces the same result as a cable release that uses a plunger – remote firing of the shutter button.

B setting
This is one of the most useful shutter speeds for the lowlight photographer. It is found below the slowest shutter speed on the shutter speed dial. Selecting B opens the shutter for as long as the shutter button is pressed, and releasing it immediately closes the shutter. It's the basis for long night-time exposures and for open flash photography (see right).

Backlight button
A feature that is used to compensate for excessive lighting behind a subject, which would otherwise fool an automatic exposure system into giving an incorrect exposure.

Ball and socket head
An adjustable platform on top of a tripod that is able to position the camera freely and hold it in a rigid position.

Beanbag
Dried seeds or beans encased in a small cloth, velvet or plastic bag. The fact that its shape can be moulded makes it an ideal steadying support for a camera or lens in the absence of a tripod.

Cable release
A cable with a plunger at one end, and connected to a camera's shutter button at the other end. This enables the camera to be controlled from a distance. There are manual and electronic cable releases and they come in a variety of lengths. A bulb, or air, release is a cable release which is controlled by air via a manually squeezable rubber bulb.

CdS
Abbreviation for Cadmium Sulphide, a light-sensitive element used in light meters for calculating exposures.

Chestpod
A type of modified camera support that rests against the chest for steadying purposes. Some types have a support base that is modelled on a rifle butt.

Compensating filters
Special coloured filters that are used to compensate for colour shifts that can occur when using film for very long exposures or under artificial lighting.

Dedicated flash
A flashgun with exposure and performance features that are designed to work with a specific camera brand or range.

Dioptre correction
A feature found in some camera viewfinders that enables the optical focus of the viewfinder to be adjusted to suit spectacle wearers.

Evaluative flash metering
A feature of a dedicated flashgun that is able to provide a flash exposure based on the readings supplied by a camera's evaluative metering system.

Evaluative metering
An SLR metering method that provides an exposure based on meter readings taken from different parts of a scene and then calculated to give an average reading.

Exposure bracketing
Taking several shots of the same subject but at different exposure settings, above as well as below the correct exposure setting. This gives the photographer a range of options to choose from as the so-called 'correct' exposure setting may not always be as effective with certain subjects or lighting situations. Some high-end SLRs have auto-exposure bracketing which allows the user to set the camera to take a series of shots automatically at pre-selected settings.

Exposure latitude
The extent of under -1 or overexposure of which a film is capable while still providing an acceptable image. Slide films tend to have a narrow exposure latitude with a working range of at most one stop either side of the correct exposure setting. Colour print films tend to have a wider exposure latitude, typically providing acceptable images at up to two stops either side of the correct exposure.

Exposure value (EV)
Any aperture and shutter speed combination that is able to provide a correct exposure. The EV range is an indication of the exposure capabilities of a particular camera or light meter.

Film grain
The texture of film emulsion. A characteristic of fast or pushed film is that the grain becomes more noticeable. This gives a distinctive quality to images.

Flash bracket
An attachable arm that fits on to a camera and provides support for an external flashgun. Some flash brackets are adjustable so as to increase the distance between them and the camera for more

versatile flash illumination.

Flash sync socket
The flash synchronisation socket enables an external flashgun to be connected directly to the camera body via a cable rather than via the camera's flash hotshoe. It is most often used in conjunction with the flash bracket.

Flash sync speed
The shutter speed that synchronises the camera's shutter with the flashgun. Depending on the camera in use, typical flash sync speeds are 1/30 sec, 1/60 sec, 1/90 sec, 1/125 sec, and 1/250 sec. The flash synchronises with the flash sync speed and also with any shutter speed slower than it. On an SLR camera, using a shutter speed faster than the flash sync speed will cause part of the image to be blacked out.

Guide number
The guide number of a flashgun indicates its power output. The higher the guide number the more powerful the flashgun. A flashgun with a guide number of 25, used with ISO 100 film and with an aperture of, say, f5.6 will be able to give adequate illumination for a subject that is around 4m away. Built-in flashguns typically have a GN of around 12. The GN of external flashguns is usually around 25 while some can be as high as 90.

Hotshoe flash sync adaptor
Most flash sync sockets are found on the camera body, but others are found on special attachable adaptors that fit into the camera's hotshoe.

Image stabilisers
Some cameras and lenses have special electronic circuitry that is able to sense and subdue accidental movement or shake to produce a blur-free picture.

Long duration flash
See Slow speed flash sync

Mercury vapour
A type of street lighting that looks white in real life but appears as greenish-blue when photographed using normal film.

Neutral density filter
Sometimes the light reaching the film needs to be dramatically reduced, beyond even the limits of the camera's exposure system. For this a neutral density filter is used. This filter darkens the image seen through the lens without affecting the colours. Neutral density filters come in different strengths and are sometimes necessary for long exposures involving bright light-source subjects.

NiCad batteries
NiCad stands for Nickel Cadmium which is a component used in special rechargeable batteries.

Open flash technique
This technique is commonly used for artificially lighting dark and complex interiors with flash. The shutter speed is set to B, then a series of flashes is fired while the shutter is open.

Reciprocity law failure
Reciprocity law failure happens when lighting conditions go beyond the capabilities of a film and it is unable to cope. The results are usually false colours and variations in lighting.

Ringflash
A ringflash is a special flashgun in which the flash is ring-shaped. This provides virtually shadow-free lighting and is useful for close ups. It is also sometimes used in some portraiture. A telltale sign that a ringflash has been used is the appearance of ring-shaped highlights in an image.

Selenium
A light-sensitive element used in some light meters. It has now largely been replaced by more sensitive SPD systems of light-reading.

Shoulder pod
See Chestpod.

SPD
Silicon Photo Diode, a light-sensitive element used in light meters.

Slow speed flash sync
With this feature, seen on some some high-end cameras, the duration of the flash corresponds to selected slow shutter speeds.

Snoot
A conical device which fits over the front of a light reflector to restrict its beam and limit spill.

Spot-metering
This is a way to measure light selectively from a small part of a subject. It is used for fine-tuned exposure readings, or to work out an average general reading.

Strobe flash
This special type of flash unit lets out a rapid succession of powerful but brief flash emissions. It's ideal for capturing quickly-moving action subjects showing them as a selection of frozen images all on the same frame of film. N.B. In some countries a normal flashgun is often called a 'strobe'.

Table-top tripod
A mini tripod that can support a compact camera or a small SLR. Some mini tripods can be adjusted for use as chestpods.

Tripod clamp
A powerful clamp with a tripod platform, which can be clamped on to rigid objects such as railings or fences.

Warming filters
Filters that provide warmer colouring to an image usually yellow or orange. Often used to neutralise the cool blue effects of certain types of daylight such as early morning light.

Pascal Baetens was born in 1963. He photographs for European fashion and glamour magazines. His first book 'The Fragile Touch' (ISBN 1-898998-140) is filled with his moody black and white nudes. It was published by The Erotic Print Society, London in 1999. Pascal Baetens' work has been largely exhibited in Europe.
Address Studio P.J.J.
W. Coosemansstraat 122
B 3010 Kessel-Lo
Belgium
Phone +32 16 258411
Fax +32 16 258470
Mobile +32 75 390244
Email pascal.baetens@advalvas.be

Eric Boutilier-Brown has been pursuing his passion for photography since 1986 and began working with the nude in 1988. Since 1995 the major focus of his creative output has been his website Evolving Vision. Eric works predominantly in black and white.
Address 3-2331 Creighton Street
Halifax NS
B3K 3R8
Canada
Phone +1 902 425 5091
Fax +1 902 425 2057
Email ebb@hfx.andara.com
Website http://ebb.ns.ca

Rene de Carufel A freelance professional photographer with 20 years of experience working out of a fully equipped commercial studio in Montreal, Rene de Carufel specialises in several areas: corporate, annual reports, industrial, advertising, table-top, digital imaging, fine art, artistic nude, landscape, people, lifestyle, celebrities, portraits and travel. Rene studied photography in the USA and film production at Concordia University in Montreal. He has been producer, director and Director of Photography on a number of films and videos. Some recent clients include Bell Canada, Nexacor, Uniglobal, Leader Canada Inc., Government of Quebec, Lawson Mardon Margo Inc., St. Lawrence Cement Ltd., Pharmaprix, Bacardi, Praxair.
Address 2551 De Chateauguay St, No. 302
Montreal
Quebec
H3K 3K4
Canada
Phone +1 514 935 6808
Fax +1 514 932 8693
Email rdc@odyssee.net

Michael Engman is a self-taught photographer who works in advertising and reportage for magazines. He likes experimenting in the studio darkroom where shape and colour are most important.
Address Fotograf Michael Engman
Box 177S-881
24 Solleftea
Sweden
Phone & Fax +46 620 68 38 38
Email engman@sfoto.se
Website www.engmanbild.nu

Michèle Francken Besides publicity and fashion photography, Michèle Francken also specialises in creative portraits and still life. Her images are featured in several exhibitions both in her native Belgium and internationally.
Address Vlaanderenstraat 5
19000 Gent
Belgium
Phone +32 9 225 43 08
Fax +32 9 224 21 32

Marc Jaffe has owned a photolab and photography studio since 1988. He specialises in light-painting and corporate imagery. He is currently pursuing a parallel career as an Internet designer. His work can be seen at www.marcjaffe.com
Address 12 Spruce Road
South Salem
NY 10590
USA
Phone +1 914 715 6969
Fax +1 914 763 6510
Email marc@marcjaffe.com
Website www.marcjaffe.com

Catherine McIntyre specialises in digital compositions created by computer. Her background was in classical illustration but a Masters degree in photography showed new technical possibilities, particularly those offered by digital effects software packages. Her first book 'Deliquescence' is published by Pohlmann Press.
Address Catherine McIntyre Digital Illustrator
8 Park Avenue
Dundee
Tayside
DD4 6PW
Scotland
Phone & Fax +44 1382 860907
Email c.mcintyre@cableinet.co.uk
Website http://wkweb5.cableinet.co.uk/c.mcintyre/home.html

Skip Middleton has no formal education in photography, so his photographic education has come from studying the great photographers. His main influences have been Edward Weston, Walker Evans, Imogen Cunningham and George Hurrell.
Address Shadowcatcher Imagery

1651 S. Juniper Street No. 95
Escondido
CA 92025
USA
Phone +1 760 743 5412
Fax +1 760 743 6130
Email shadowcatcher@home.com
Website http://members.tripod.com/-shadowcatcherimagery/index.htm

Bob Norris moved to Paris in the 1980s. He worked as an assistant in Studio Daguerre and also assisted Helmut Newton and Sarah Moon. Today he works for Marie Claire, Biba and Vogue.
Address Bob Norris Photographer
18 Rue Georges Thill
75019 Paris
France
Phone +44 208 870 3462 Mark Gibson, UK Agent . +33 153 53 9191 Angela de Bona, French Agent.

Bryan Remer is a Bay Area photographer, a stockbroker in San Franscisco, and a former US Navy carrier pilot. In developing his style he has drawn from inspiration from the works of photographers Ruth Bernard, Lucien Clergue, Robert Farber, David Hamilton, Sam Haskins and Jeanloup Sief. He and his wife Kim live with their two shih-tzus in the Oakland Hills.
Address PO Box 2634
San Francisco
CA 94126
USA
Phone +1 510 339 8575
Email photos@remer.com
Website http://www.remer.com

Kevin Roberts lives on the Space Coast of Florida. At college he studied theatre and dance before a motorcycle accident pushed him towards software engineering and corporate America. One day breaking free of corporate restraints, he's never looked back.
Address Intimate Images® Photography
1433 Highland Ave.
Melbourne
FL 32935
USA
Phone +1 407 242 8418
Studio +1 757 583 0200
Agent Fax +1 407 242 9345
Email photoguy@intimateimages.net

Sally Russ began her career as a professional photographer in 1984, photographing show business personalities, actors and models. Her transition to becoming a fine art photographer occurred gradually and quite naturally as some of her clients consented to become her models for more artistic studies. Sally discovered that they enjoyed being photographed as much as she enjoyed photographing them, and her ability to connect with them on a personal level has allowed her to produce very intimate, quietly erotic images.
Address Box 1593
Winter Park,
Florida 32790
USA
Phone +1 407 629 1910
Fax +1 407 629 1939
Email sally@sallyruss.com